MY COFFEE-C

MEDITATIONS

Coffeetime in Autumn

Bible-based Reflections for Each Day of the Season

ROGER ELLSWORTH

This edition 2022 Coffeetime in Autumn
ISBN 978-1-63342-284-1

Shepherd Press
P.O. Box 24
Wapwallopen, PA 18660

www.shepherdpress.com

www.mycoffeecup meditations.com

www.rogerellsworth.org

Coffeetime in Autumn

Bible-based Reflections for Each Day of the Season

Purpose

My Coffee Cup Meditations are short, easy-to-read, engagingly presented devotions based on the Bible, the Word of God. Each reading takes a single idea or theme and develops it in a thought-provoking way so that you are inspired to consider the greatness of God, the relevance of the good news of the life, death, resurrection, and coming-again of Jesus, and are better equipped for life in this world and well prepared for the world to come.

www.mycoffeecupmeditations.com

https://www.facebook.com/MyCoffeeCupMeditations/

We hope you will enjoy these Bible-based meditations. We would love to hear from you, so please send us a note to tell us what you think—which ones you liked most, and how they made a difference in your life or in the life of a family member, friend, or work associate.

To reach us online, go to
www.mycoffeecupmeditations.com/contact

We offer quantity discounts for bulk quantity purchases.
Contact us for more details.

Be sure to collect each of the four volumes in this series!

Coffeetime in Winter: 978-1-63342-281-0
Coffeetime in Spring: 978-1-63342-282-7
Coffeetime in Summer: 978-1-63342-283-4
Coffeetime in Autumn: 978-1-63342-284-1

About the Authors

Roger Ellsworth is a retired pastor, active in ministry and writing, who lives in Jackson, Tennessee. He and his wife, Sylvia, love the message of the Bible, and they enjoy sharing the wonderful counsel of the Word of God in language that ordinary people can understand and appreciate. Roger has written numerous books on the Christian faith, and has exercised a preaching ministry for over fifty years.

Roger and Sylvia have two sons, Tim and Martyn, who have also contributed devotions to this volume.

Introduction: All About this Series

FROM GOD'S WORD, THE BIBLE...

Most assuredly, I say to you, he who does not enter the sheepfold by the door, but climbs up some other way, the same is a thief and a robber. But he who enters by the door is the shepherd of the sheep. To him the door-keeper opens, and the sheep hear his voice; and he calls his own sheep by name and leads them out. And when he brings out his own sheep, he goes before them; and the sheep follow him, for they know his voice. Yet they will by no means follow a stranger, but will flee from him, for they do not know the voice of strangers.

JOHN 10:1-6

What you have here is the fourth part of what was produced as a big book—twelve books all in one, in fact. The idea of connecting enjoying coffee and reading the Bible devotionally happened early in 2017 when I wrote the first book in what became a series of *My Coffee-Cup Meditations*.

Tender shepherds take the best care of their sheep. They lead them to where there is good, nutritious grass, a supply of fresh water, shade from fierce heat, and he is sure to defend them from animals that would prey on them. The Lord Jesus Christ is the Good Shepherd. He tends His sheep, believers He has redeemed by His work on the cross. And He feeds them from the rich treasures of His Word, the Bible. God's Word is nourishing food when it is regularly imbibed through reading, reflection, and study. Christians must read the Bible, and so a daily devotional book can significantly help in this regard.

Early mornings are very predictable for lots and lots of Christians. Roll out of bed, turn on the coffee pot, pour a cup, settle into a favorite chair and enjoy what is called "the daily devotional." This usually consists of reading a passage from the Bible and a selection from a devotional book. It concludes with prayer.

Christians who follow this pattern can go through a good bit of devotional material as the years go by. So they are always looking for new material—something to go along with their Bible and their coffee.

Hoping that I could be helpful in supplying the need for more devotional material, I gathered up some articles I had written and put them in a book—*A Dog and a Clock*. The idea was to supply brothers and sisters in Christ with enough devotions to carry them through one month. That quickly led to another book—*The Thumbs Up Man*—to carry "devotion-doers" through another month and then another.

You can guess what happened after three or four books came out. There are twelve months in the year. So why not provide enough books to cover a year? So off we went and out the books came until there were finally twelve books, each with thirty-one readings! Since these books were designed to go with the Bible and a good cup of coffee, it seemed right to call them *My Coffee-Cup Meditations*. Thanks to my good friends Jim and Sue Holmes for that suggestion! And thanks to my wife, Sylvia, and my sons, Tim and Martyn, for contributing some chapters along the way.

Then came the idea of producing the books together, so that there would be enough readings for a whole year, and with some left over, as not all months have thirty-one days. So the result is that we combined all twelve of the books into one big one: *The Big Book of Coffee Cup Meditations*! That way, people would be able to read from whichever month they wished to at any time in the year—and never have too few days in the month, because there would always be thirty-one readings in each month!

As we thought and prayed about how to present these books in yet another format, the idea of Bible readings for each of the seasons of the year came to mind: Coffeetime in Winter, Spring, Summer, and Fall. And so it is that you are holding the fourth of the set of four books in your hand!

One of my main concerns in writing these books was to cause the gospel of our Lord Jesus Christ to shine. It's wrong to think that the gospel is for unbelievers only. Believers need the gospel! We need to be reminded again and again of the greatness of what our Lord Jesus Christ did for us in His life, death, resurrection, and ascension. The more we ponder the gospel and the more deeply we ponder it, the more we will find our hearts flooded with gratitude, and the more willing we will be to faithfully serve Him.

My Coffee-Cup Meditations are published for you with the hope that you will read the devotions, enjoy them, and, most of all, find that you are inspired to consider the greatness of God, the relevance of the good news of the life, death, resurrection, and coming-again of Jesus, and are better equipped for life in this world and well prepared for the world to come.

And don't forget to pour that cup of coffee!

THE MONTH OF OCTOBER

Apples of Gold in Silver Settings

... And 30 Other Bible-Based Meditations

I've seen gold, and I've seen silver, but I have never seen apples of gold in silver settings. My initial reaction is that such apples in such settings must reflect both tremendous value and exquisite beauty. There are words like that—words of tremendous value and exquisite beauty! And we can possess them even though they were all spoken so very long ago. We can possess them by reading the reports of them in the Bible and by reflecting deeply on what we have read.

October 1

Apples of Gold in Silver Settings

From God's Word, the Bible...

A word fitly spoken is like apples of gold
In settings of silver.

Proverbs 25:11

A word "fitly spoken" is the appropriate word. It's the right word for the occasion. It's the word that fits. It's the word that causes us to say: "Yes, that's it. There's nothing else to say."

The Bible reports many fitly spoken words. All of the Bible's words are true and significant, but I'm talking about those instances in which the Bible actually reports what someone had to say to another person or to other people.

In the readings that follow, we will notice some words that God the Father spoke. Fit words they were! We will also notice many of the words that the Lord Jesus spoke. Wonderful words indeed! There will be a reading on a word that the Holy Spirit actually spoke as well as some readings on words that angels spoke. And, of course, we will want to notice some fitly words spoken by human beings.

I trust that each of these readings will seem to you to be as an apple of gold in a setting of silver.

I've seen gold, and I've seen silver, but I have never seen apples of gold in silver settings. My initial reaction is that such apples in such settings must reflect both tremendous value and exquisite beauty.

There are words like that. Words of tremendous value and exquisite beauty! And we can possess them even though they were all spoken so very long ago. We can possess them by reading the reports of them in the Bible and by reflecting deeply on what we have read. If we don't read these things and reflect on them, we are depriving ourselves of both their value and their beauty.

For words to be like apples of gold in silver settings, they have to deal with matters of great importance. One can speak a fit word even when trivial matters are being discussed, but that surely wouldn't qualify as an apple of gold in a setting of silver.

The words that will receive our attention in the readings that follow are truly valuable because they all have some connection with the one matter of supreme importance, namely, God's plan of salvation. We might say they all have some connection with the matter of receiving eternal life. No other words can compare to these. Simon Peter, who so often said the wrong thing, said exactly the right thing when he spoke these words to Jesus: "Lord, to whom shall we go? You have the words of eternal life" (John 6:68).

That was certainly a word fitly spoken. It was an apple of gold in a silver setting.

In the early 1870s, Fleming H. Revell (Dwight Moody's brother-in-law) was in the process of launching a Christian publication that was to be called *Words of Life*. Mr. Revell persuaded Philip Bliss to write a hymn that would be appropriate for the first issue. In 1874, that issue was released with this hymn from Bliss:

Sing them over again to me,
Wonderful words of life;
Let me more of their beauty see,
Wonderful words of life;
Words of life and beauty,
Teach me faith and duty:
Beautiful words, wonderful words,
Wonderful words of life;
Beautiful words, wonderful words,
Wonderful words of life.

A few short months after writing that hymn, Philip Bliss and his wife entered into the life of which he had so often written, dying in a train wreck in Ohio in December of 1876.

Because Philip Bliss' hymn celebrated the wonderful words that lead us to eternal life, I would call it an apple of gold in a setting of silver.

Bliss was only thirty-eight when he died. This life is so very unpredictable. It can end very quickly and plunge us out into eternity. How very many there are who are speeding toward it without giving any thought to it!

In *The Pilgrim's Progress*, John Bunyan has the pilgrim leaving the City of Destruction, crying as he runs down the path: "Eternal life! Eternal life!" We would do well to do as the pilgrim did. We would do well to prize eternal life above all else. We would do well to read and heed the words that God, angels, and men have spoken about eternal life. Like apples of gold in settings of silver, they are words of enormous value and beauty.

October 2

God Speaks to Satan

From God's Word, the Bible...

"And I will put enmity
Between you and the woman,
And between your seed and her Seed;
He shall bruise your head,
And you shall bruise His heel."

Genesis 3:15

Everything now seemed so bleak! So grim! Adam and Eve thought that disobeying God would bring them happiness. It didn't. They didn't realize what they had done. Through their disobedience they had essentially broken their friendship with God and formed a new friendship with Satan—a ghastly friendship!

God could have left it that way. He could have let this new friendship stand. But God came after His disobedient creatures, found them, and announced that He was going to break their new friendship. He would destroy their friendship with the devil and restore them to friendship with Himself.

It's all recorded right there in Genesis 3:15. God says to Satan (who had appeared as a serpent):

I will put enmity
Between you and the woman. . . .

Enmity is the opposite of friendship. Satan had used the woman to destroy friendship with God (vv. 1-6); God would use her to restore that friendship.

How would God use the woman to restore friendship with Himself? Through her would come the "Seed." Notice the singular. God would restore sinners to friendship with Himself through one person being born of a woman. The fact that God was referring to one person is established when the Lord goes on to say: "He shall. . ."

Who is this person who would be born of a woman for the purpose of undoing what the devil had done? It is none other than the Lord Jesus Christ (Gal. 4:4). Amazing thing! He, the Second Person of the Trinity, would actually be born of a woman! He would take our humanity!

What we have here is God saying to Satan: "You used the man I put here to destroy My friendship. I'm going to send another Man, another Adam, to undo what you have done. You have succeeded with My first Adam. Let's see how you do with the Second Adam."

How Satan hated this announcement! How he hated Jesus, the Seed of the woman! And how he stirred up hostility against Him!

Coming to this earth in our humanity was certainly an amazing thing, but it wasn't enough to actually restore sinners to friendship with God. To do that, Jesus had to die on the cross, and, yes, the cross is found here in Genesis 3:15. It's in these words:

He shall bruise your head,
And you shall bruise His heel.

The hatred of Satan for Jesus would culminate in Jesus being crucified. That cross looked to be a stunning victory for Satan. Jesus had come, and Satan had won! That's how it appeared. But Satan's "victory" was only the bruising of Jesus' heel. That cross which appeared to be Satan's victory was in fact Jesus' victory. It consisted of Jesus bringing His bruised heel down with crushing force on Satan's head!

How did Jesus' death on the cross defeat Satan? What happened there to break the friendship of sinners with Satan and to restore them to friendship with God? It paid the penalty of sin. Sin is the chain that binds sinners to Satan. What a friendship—one that uses a chain!

Jesus died on the cross to pay the penalty for sinners. His death broke the chain. With sin's penalty paid, Satan no longer had the chain with which to bind sinners to himself in "friendship."

Adam and Eve were restored to life's true friendship, friendship with God, by looking forward in faith to the coming and dying of the Lord Jesus Christ.

Adam's sin caused all of his descendants to be born as sinners. All of us come into this world in a state of friendship with Satan and alienation toward God. But it doesn't have to stay that way. We can enter into friendship with God by looking in faith to the redeeming work of the Lord Jesus. Adam and Eve looked forward to Christ, we look backward to Christ, but being saved has always been, is and always will be, a matter of looking to Christ.

If I were asked to make a list of the most amazing words ever spoken, I would have to begin with the words God spoke in Genesis 3:15. I would like to have been there to have heard those words. They announced the way for me to be forgiven of my sins and restored to friendship with God. What wonderful words! But I didn't have to hear them when they were spoken because I can hear them now as I read this verse. For that, I'm thankful.

October 3

The Son Speaks to the Father

From God's Word, the Bible...

Sacrifice and offering You did not desire;
My ears You have opened.
Burnt offering and sin offering You did not require.
Then I said, "Behold, I come;
In the scroll of the book it is written of me.
I delight to do Your will, O my God,
And Your law is within my heart."

Psalm 40:6-8

Have you ever wished you could have listened in on a highly significant conversation? Have you ever wished you could have been a fly on the wall in the innermost chambers of highly influential people as they discussed crucial matters? These verses make us that fly on the wall. They enable us to hear one side of the greatest of all conversations.

David, the king of Israel, reports this half of the conversation to us. But while he wrote these words, they aren't really his words. The Spirit of God carried David to such a high level that he was enabled to write the words of the Lord Jesus Himself. David was here serving as the mouthpiece of the Messiah.

To whom did the Messiah speak these words? There can be no doubt about that. They are addressed to God the Father. Note the phrase "O my God" in verse 8.

The Father had given His Son a task. This was no small task! It was to accomplish that work which all the sacrifices of the Old Testament era could never accomplish. Those sacrifices, while ordained by God, could only paint a picture of salvation for sinners. They could never actually provide it. The work of salvation was still awaiting the doing. And now we have the Lord Jesus declaring that He was coming to do the work. He says to the Father: "Behold, I come."

When did Jesus speak these words? The answer that leaps to mind is when He was ready to leave the courts of heaven to enter this realm in our humanity.

It should be plain to us that the three persons of the Trinity were united on this matter of redeeming sinners. It was the Holy Spirit who prompted David to write about redemption. It was the Father's will to save sinners by sending His Son. And the Son didn't reluctantly, grudgingly take up the work. Not for a moment! He says:

I delight to do Your will, O my God,
And Your law is within my heart.
(v. 8)

What does it mean to be a sinner? It means we are law breakers. We refuse to keep God's laws and insist on going our own way. Our law breaking disqualifies us from entering heaven because God demands that we be perfectly righteous to enter there. Thank God for Jesus. The law we so deeply despise and so frequently break, He embraced with all of His heart. And He perfectly kept it. In doing so, He provided for us that perfect righteousness which God demands.

After living that life of perfect obedience, Jesus went to the cross to receive the penalty of our law breaking. Here is the gospel in a nutshell—Jesus got our sins so that all who believe in Him may have His righteousness.

What is this "scroll of the Book" which Jesus mentions? Some think it refers to the Old Testament, all of which points forward to the coming of Christ and the work of salvation that He would achieve. Others think this scroll takes us all the way back to that time even before the world began when the Father, the Son, and the Holy Spirit entered into agreement with each other about the work of redemption and wrote it all down.

It's really not necessary for us to choose between these two possibilities because each is true. It is true that the three persons of the Trinity agreed with each other on the details of redemption before the world began. And it is true that the Old Testament prophesied the work of Christ. Let's refuse to choose, and let's rejoice in both!

What a conversation we have depicted in these verses! The Father must have said: "Son, here is the work of redemption that You must do!" And the Son responded: "Yes, Father, I will take up the work. I will gladly and fully do it to the last detail."

Jesus' side of this conversation expressed His commitment to our salvation. Because of His commitment—one He didn't have to make—all who repent of their sins and trust in Him have forgiveness for their sins and eternal life.

October 4

An Angel Speaks to Joseph

FROM GOD'S WORD, THE BIBLE...

But while he thought about these things, behold, an angel of the Lord appeared to him in a dream, saying, "Joseph, son of David, do not be afraid to take to you Mary your wife, for that which is conceived in her is of the Holy Spirit. And she will bring forth a Son, and you shall call His name Jesus, for He will save His people from their sins."

MATTHEW 1:20-21

Mary was pregnant, and her fiancé Joseph was perplexed. The child wasn't his. Assuming Mary had been unfaithful to him, he was inclined to break their engagement quietly, that is, without subjecting Mary to the legal procedures of that time.

Then everything changed for Joseph in an instant. An angel suddenly appeared to him in a dream to offer an explanation and to give an instruction.

The explanation had to do with Mary's pregnancy. It was unique. There had not been one like this before. The angel said: ". . . that which is conceived in her is of the Holy Spirit" (v. 20).

The instruction had to do with the naming of the One who was to be born. The angel said to Joseph: ". . . you shall call His name Jesus, for He will save His people from their sins" (v. 21).

I love the name "Jesus" because it means "salvation," and this I know about myself: I need salvation. What is it that I need to be saved from? The angel made it clear. I need to be saved from my sins. And what I have said about myself is true of everyone. We are all sinners (Rom. 3:23), and we all need to be saved from our sins.

Jesus came to this earth for the express purpose of providing salvation for sinners, and there would be no such salvation had He not come.

Yes, Jesus provides an example for us on the matter of how we should live, but that wasn't the primary reason that He came. Jesus was certainly a marvelous teacher, but He didn't come to only be a teacher. Jesus came to be the Savior. Any explanation for Him other than that comes woefully short of the truth about the Lord Jesus.

To say that Jesus came to this earth to save sinners is to say that He came to pay the penalty that those sinners deserve. God's holy character precludes Him from forgiving sinners without that penalty being paid. God would sin against Himself if He were to ignore the penalty that He Himself had pronounced on sin. So the huge question was this: how could God at one and the same time carry out the penalty that He had pronounced on sinners and let those very same sinners go free? To put it another way, how could God both punish and not punish sinners? Or, to put it yet another way, how could God simultaneously satisfy His justice that demanded payment for sin and His grace that demanded release for sinners? Enormous dilemma!

Now you know why I love the name "Jesus." He is the answer to God's dilemma. On the cross, He received the penalty that God's justice required. What a penalty it was! It was the penalty of eternal separation from God, and Jesus experienced that on the cross. That's why He cried: "My God, My God, why have You forsaken Me?" (Matt. 27:46).

Because He was God, an infinite person, He could receive an eternity's worth of wrath in a finite measure of time. Amazing!

Justice looked on the cross of Jesus and clapped its hands in approval because the demand that it made against sinners was fully carried out. But grace looked on that same cross and clapped its hands as well for this reason: because Jesus had paid the penalty, there was no penalty left for those sinners who trust in Him. Justice and grace met in Jesus.

Now you see the reason I love the name "Jesus." But I have to say there's another word that I love in the angel's announcement. It is the word "will." That's a definite word. It doesn't allow for uncertainty. Jesus was coming to this earth to provide salvation for sinners, and He would succeed in that work. Nothing would stop Him.

I would have enjoyed hearing the angel speak his words of explanation and instruction to Joseph because those words pertain to something that pertains to me—salvation from my sins. There is nothing greater to be found, and it's all found in Jesus.

We have heard the joyful sound:
Jesus saves! Jesus saves!
Spread the tidings all around:
Jesus saves! Jesus saves!

October 5

The Father Speaks from Heaven

FROM GOD'S WORD, THE BIBLE...

And suddenly a voice came from heaven, saying, "This is My beloved Son, in whom I am well pleased."

While he was still speaking, behold, a bright cloud overshadowed them; and suddenly a voice came out of the cloud, saying, "This is My beloved Son, in whom I am well pleased. Hear Him!"

"Father, glorify Your name." Then a voice came from heaven, saying, "I have both glorified it and will glorify it again."

MATTHEW 3:17; 17:5; JOHN 12:28

Three times! That's how often the Father spoke audibly from heaven during His Son's earthly ministry as recorded in the Gospels.

The first of these instances occurred immediately after Jesus was baptized by John the Baptist in the Jordan River.

John's baptism was intended to be an outward expression or picture of genuine repentance for sin (Matt. 3:6,8,11). Jesus showed up one day and asked John to baptize Him. So we're faced with a mystery. If John's baptism was intended to signal repentance of sin, why would Jesus, who never sinned, need to be baptized?

John the Baptist was certainly shocked by Jesus' request. He knew the truth about Jesus. He knew that He was the spotless Lamb of God who had no sin. If there was no sin in Jesus, there was no need for repentance, and, therefore, no need for baptism.

But while Jesus Himself had no sin, He came to save sinners. In order to save sinners, He had to be their substitute. He had to be the sin-bearer. By standing with John in the waters of the Jordan, Jesus was identifying with the sinners He came to save. He was presenting Himself as their substitute. He was standing with them in their sinfulness, even though He had no sins.

It's interesting that each Person of the Trinity was there at the Jordan River. Jesus, the Son, was there to be baptized. The Spirit of God was there to descend upon Him (Matt. 3:16), and the Father was there to express His approval of His Son (Matt. 3:17). The Father had sent His Son to take the place of sinners as their sin-bearer. So the Father was pleased to see the baptism of His Son.

The second time the Father spoke from heaven was also in approval of His Son. On a mountaintop with three of His disciples, Jesus was suddenly "transfigured before them" (Matt. 17:2) and stood there with Moses and Elijah (Matt. 17:3). We might say Jesus temporarily pulled back the robe of His humanity so the glory of His deity could be clearly seen.

Jesus, Moses, and Elijah didn't simply appear together. They also talked. And what did they talk about? Luke tells us that they "spoke of His decease which He was about to accomplish at Jerusalem" (Luke 9:31).

The fact that Moses, the representative of the Law, and Elijah, the representative of the prophets, spoke to Jesus about His upcoming death shows us that His death fulfilled both the Law and the prophets. His death wasn't merely something that would *happen* to Him. It was something that He would "accomplish." It was the work that He had come to do, and He would do it.

The baptism of Jesus had to do with the cross, and the Transfiguration had to do with the cross. And each time, God the Father spoke from heaven to express His approval. The Father and the Son were in agreement on the work of the cross. The Father sent the Son to die for sinners, and Jesus came to do as the Father willed.

The third time that the Father spoke from heaven during Jesus' earthly ministry is reported in John's Gospel. On this occasion, the Father spoke in response to Jesus' prayer: "Father, glorify Your name" (John 12:28).

The Father spoke to say that He had both glorified His name and would glorify it again.

We should note that this instance of the Father speaking was also connected with Jesus' death on the cross (John 12:23-24). We might expect Jesus to say: "The hour has come that the Son of Man should be crucified." Instead He said the hour had come for Him to be "glorified."

That shameful, ignominious cross would bring glory to both the Son and the Father. The glory of what Jesus was going to do there would be far greater than the shame He would suffer there. That cross would display the justice, the grace, and the wisdom of God, and, in doing so, would glorify God. That cross would save sinners, and, in doing so, would bring glory to God. The glory of the cross is greater than the sin that made it necessary.

It would certainly have been an awesome thing to hear the Father speak from heaven on those three occasions. But it is an even greater thing to embrace by faith the cross of Christ that received the approval of the Father.

October 6

The First Words of Jesus' Ministry

FROM GOD'S WORD, THE BIBLE...

Now after John was put in prison, Jesus came to Galilee, preaching the gospel of the kingdom of God, and saying, "The time is fulfilled, and the kingdom of God is at hand. Repent, and believe in the gospel."

MARK 1:14-15

After He was tempted in the wilderness, the Lord Jesus went into Galilee where He began "preaching the kingdom of God."

With that message, the Lord struck the keynote for His entire ministry. The four Gospels include over a hundred references to this matter of the kingdom of God. This was the very centerpiece of Jesus' teaching and preaching, and of all that He did.

As we read the opening words of Jesus' ministry, we should be impressed with *the definiteness of them.* Jesus came preaching (v. 14). The word "preaching" takes us to the days in which a king would make important announcements through his herald. The herald would blow a trumpet to get the attention of the people and then announce the news.

This type of thing was always definite. Martyn Lloyd-Jones observes:

> A herald does not make an uncertain announcement, or get up and blow his trumpet and say, "Listen, we do not quite know what's happening nor what is going to take place, but, well, we only hope that something is going to happen!" That is not heralding! [1]

Our time is very hostile to definiteness in religion. We welcome it in other areas. We want our physicians to be definite and precise in their treatment of us. We want our mechanics to be definite and precise in repairing our cars. But we don't like definiteness in religion because with it come clear responsibilities and painful guilt when we fail in those responsibilities. We want everyone, no matter what he believes and how he behaves, to be right on this matter of religion.

The Lord Jesus came with a very definite message about the kingdom of God. He didn't come saying: "All opinions are equally valid on this matter of God's kingdom. Everyone is right, and no one is wrong."

The very fact that Jesus came preaching indicates that His message about the kingdom was very definite and precise.

1 D. Martyn Lloyd-Jones, *The Kingdom of God*, Crossway Books, 1992, p. 12.

We should also take note of *the element of good news in Jesus' announcement.*

What Jesus had to say about the kingdom of God was indescribably wonderful. What made it so? The kingdom of God refers to His sovereign rule over His people. It is that rule that frees them from the rule of sin, achieves their complete salvation, makes them part of the community of faith, and conveys them to eternal glory.

We can't appreciate how good this news is until we realize that we don't come into this world as part of God's kingdom, but rather as part of Satan's kingdom, which is the kingdom of sin, darkness, and eternal ruin.

To get into God's kingdom, we must be taken out of Satan's. The good news is this: through Christ, God takes sinners out of Satan's kingdom and makes them citizens of His own.

A third element in Jesus' proclamation of God's kingdom is *His indispensable role in it.*

Jesus came saying that His presence meant God's kingdom was "at hand." That didn't mean that it didn't exist before this. God was delivering people from their sins and sovereignly ruling over them before Jesus came. If that hadn't been true, the people who lived before Jesus came were hopelessly lost. God's kingdom was operating in the Old Testament era but in a borrowed sense, that is, borrowed against the future. People were saved by looking forward in faith to what God would eventually do in His Son to deal with their sin. In Mark 1:15, Jesus was declaring that there was no more need to look forward to the coming of the Savior—He was the Savior! He had come to break Satan's rule over sinners and to bring them under the rule of God.

As we look back, we see that the way Jesus did this was by dying on the cross as the substitute for sinners, receiving God's wrath in their stead so they wouldn't have to receive it.

The final element in Jesus' proclamation of the kingdom is *the proper response to it*—"Repent and believe in the gospel." To repent means to turn around. It means we turn from our sins to God. To believe the gospel is to rest our hope for eternal salvation on what the Lord Jesus came to do.

Jesus certainly began His ministry with fitly spoken words. As we read them, we see them to be an "apple of gold."

October 7

"I Am the Bread of Life" (Jesus)

FROM GOD'S WORD, THE BIBLE...

And Jesus said to them, "I am the bread of life. He who comes to Me shall never hunger, and he who believes in Me shall never thirst."
"I am the bread of life."

JOHN 6:35, 48

The Bible tells us that no one ever spoke like Jesus (John 7:46). How very blessed we are to be able to read in the Gospel accounts some of the many words He spoke! While we treasure those accounts, it's okay for us to wonder what it would have been like to hear those words as they fell from Jesus' lips.

Those who are familiar with John's Gospel know that it contains seven "I am" sayings from Jesus. I sometimes wish I could hurl myself through time and hear Him make each of those claims.

The first of them Jesus stated twice: "I am the bread of life." He spoke those words to people who were obsessively concerned with physical bread. On the previous day, He miraculously multiplied bread to satisfy their hunger (vv. 1-14).

Some of that multitude followed Him to Capernaum. Always able to read men, Jesus knew the reason for their interest in Him. They wanted more bread. They were being driven by their desire for "the food which perishes" (v. 27). They were primarily interested in food that would sustain physical life. Meanwhile, they were oblivious to their far greater need, which was food that could produce and sustain spiritual and eternal life.

Jesus' message to them was plain. There is a food, which, if eaten, will produce "everlasting life" (v. 27).

Life that never ends! That's something that I can certainly use! This life passes so swiftly! The years come and go with blinding speed, and then death comes to carry us away. Henry F. Lyte got it right: "Swift to its close ebbs out life's little day."

So I'm very interested in eating that food that will give me life that will never end. What is that food? It is the Lord Jesus Christ. He is the bread of life. He came to this earth from heaven for this very reason—to give "life to the world" (v. 33).

How do we know Jesus came from heaven? All we have to do is look at the many miracles that He performed. They tell us the truth about Him.

The people to whom He was speaking in John 6 had seen Jesus miraculously multiply physical food. That alone gave them sufficient reason to believe that Jesus was from heaven and could give them eternal life. Sadly enough, they all walked away from Him (v. 66). They spurned His offer of eternal life even though they had indisputable evidence that Jesus could give it to them. Their interest in physical life crowded out interest in eternal life.

What did Jesus do to provide eternal life? To put it another way, what makes Jesus the bread that produces eternal life? He gives us the answer in these words: ". . . the bread that I shall give is My flesh, which I shall give for the life of the world" (v. 51).

Jesus was talking about His death on the cross. That is where He gave His flesh and shed His blood, and that death is the thing that makes Him the bread of life, that makes it possible for Him to give us spiritual and eternal life. By dying on the cross, Jesus dealt with the thing that keeps us from having spiritual and eternal life—sin. On the cross, He received the penalty for sin, and, in doing so, took sin out of the way so it can no longer keep us from having spiritual and eternal life.

Jesus is the bread of life by virtue of His death on the cross. But Jesus, the bread, has to be eaten. How do we "eat" Jesus? In some verses, the Lord Jesus tells us that we must eat His flesh and drink His blood if we are to have eternal life (vv. 53-58). In other verses, He tells us that we must believe in Him if we are to have eternal life (vv. 29, 35, 40, 47). The point is quite clear. To eat His flesh and drink His blood means we are to believe in Him. He used the eating and drinking as a picture of believing in Him.

Doesn't this apply only to those who are the ones who have been "given" to the Son by the Father (v. 37)? Yes. But we don't have to know that we are given before we believe. We rather have to believe and then we may know that we are among the given.

October 8

"I Am the Light of the World" (Jesus)

From God's Word, the Bible...

Then Jesus spoke to them again, saying, "I am the light of the world. He who follows Me shall not walk in darkness, but have the light of life."

John 8:12

Darkness is everywhere in the first eleven verses of John 8. Sexual immorality is here. A woman has been caught in the act of adultery. But the hypocrisy of religious leaders is here also. Isn't it interesting that they have brought the woman to Jesus, but not the man? Hatred is here also. Because these religious leaders carried a smoldering hatred for Jesus, they are trying to set a trap for Him.

Against this backdrop of darkness, Jesus makes a cheering and staggering claim. He says: "I am the light of the world."

I think I would have enjoyed hearing Jesus speak those words. I know that I need light. I need it to guide me through this dark world. But my need goes beyond that. It's not just that I live in a dark world; it's rather that the darkness lives in me. And what I'm saying about myself is true of everyone else.

The Bible tells me that sin has done a real number on us. It has affected our minds, affections, and wills. It has so darkened our minds that we don't naturally understand the things of God (1 Cor. 2:14; 2 Cor. 4:3-4). It has so degraded our affections that we constantly place them on the low things of this earth instead of on the high things of God (Mark 7:21-23). It has even deadened our wills to the point that if we are left to ourselves we can't seek God or move toward Him (Rom. 3:11).

If the darkness is to be driven from us, our minds must be enlightened, our affections elevated, and our wills energized. Jesus is the light that we need. He enables us to understand, love, and choose Him and the salvation that He came to this earth to provide for sinners.

Jesus says He is the light of the world. We shouldn't take that to mean every single person in the world enjoys the salvation Jesus came to provide. Earlier in his Gospel, the Apostle John seems to suggest that. He calls Jesus "the true Light which gives light to every man who comes into the world" (John 1:9). Some have eagerly seized those words as proof that all will eventually be saved. But it's clear from the succeeding verses (vv. 10-11) that not all receive the light of Christ. What, then, is John 1:9 telling us? It's merely affirming that the light of Christ is there for all to see. But, sadly, the fact that the light is there for all to see doesn't mean all will see it.

The light we sinners need is shining in Christ, so let's heed His words: "He who follows Me shall not walk in darkness, but have the light of life."

To follow Christ is to believe in Him as our Savior and to obey Him as our Lord. It is to take His salvation by faith and to keep His commandments out of gratitude.

The Lord promises that those who follow Him will enjoy "the light of life." The Lord Jesus graciously drives the darkness out of all who believe in Him so that they pass from spiritual death into spiritual life. And the spiritual life that they receive from the Lord in this world will finally culminate in eternal life in heaven. There in heaven we will never again witness or experience the darkness created by sin.

As we journey through this dark world, let's sing these words from Philip P. Bliss:

The whole world was lost in the darkness of sin,
The light of the world is Jesus!
Like sunshine at noonday, His glory shone in;
The light of the world is Jesus!

No darkness have we who in Jesus abide;
The light of the world is Jesus!
We walk in the light when we follow our Guide!
The Light of the world is Jesus!

Ye dwellers in darkness with sin-blinded eyes,
The Light of the world is Jesus!
Go, wash at His bidding, and light will arise;
The Light of the world is Jesus!

No need of the sunlight in Heaven we're told;
The Light of the world is Jesus!
The Lamb is the Light in the city of gold,
The Light of the world is Jesus!

Refrain:
Come to the light, 'tis shining for thee;
Sweetly the light has dawned upon me;
Once I was blind, now I can see:
The Light of the world is Jesus!

October 9

"I Am the Door" (Jesus)

FROM GOD'S WORD, THE BIBLE...

Then Jesus said to them again, "Most assuredly, I say to you, I am the door of the sheep. All who ever came before Me are thieves and robbers, but the sheep did not hear them. I am the door. If anyone enters by Me, he will be saved, and will go in and out and find pasture."

JOHN 10:7-9

I would like to have been there when Jesus said: "I am the door." I would have rejoiced in hearing that because I need a door. There's nothing that I need more. But I'm getting ahead of myself.

Two of Jesus' "I am" sayings are found in John 10. In the verses before us, Jesus claims to be "the door." Jesus also claims to be "the good shepherd" (vv. 11,14). He states each of these claims two times.

It's important to connect these two claims with the events reported in John 9. There we have Jesus healing a man born blind. Instead of rejoicing with this man, the religious leaders cast him out of the synagogue (vv. 22,34). Jesus began rebuking the religious leaders for their action in verse 41 of chapter 9, and He continues to do so in the first eighteen verses of chapter 10. The section beginning with 9:1 and ending with 10:39 is a unity and should be read as such.

By using the pictures of the door and the good shepherd, Jesus is showing these religious leaders to be false and dangerous leaders. These men claimed to be the spiritual shepherds of the people, but they proved they weren't when they excommunicated the man healed of blindness.

Nothing is more important for our own spiritual wellbeing than being able to distinguish between true and false ministers. How are we to do this? The main thing to always keep in mind is this: the true ministry has a door in it.

The door to what? Doors to be doors must open so we can have access to something. By telling those religious leaders that He, Jesus, was the door, He was claiming to be the One who give access to something of tremendous importance—salvation from sin. Jesus says: "I am the door. If anyone enters by Me, he will be saved. . ." (v. 9).

The true minister is one who has used the door himself and is now pointing others to that door and urging them to use it. And the door is Jesus. So we can say the true minister is Christ-centered. He has received Jesus as his Lord and Savior, and he now preaches salvation through Christ to others.

On the other hand, the false minister doesn't use the door. He doesn't preach the coming and the dying of the Lord Jesus as the only means of salvation. He tries to get the sheep to follow him by approaching them in some way other than Christ. The final result of this approach is death.

But it's not enough to merely say the false minister is false. He is; but it's worse than that. The false minister is also a thief. By refusing to preach Christ as the way of salvation, he actually robs people of the very thing they so desperately need. He robs them of eternal salvation. Jesus gives spiritual life; the thief deprives people of the same (v. 10).

A couple of things should be very clear to us by now. One is that we should highly prize those ministries that have the door in them. We should prize Christ-centered ministers who faithfully set before us the saving work of the Lord Jesus. The other thing is that we should avoid those ministries and ministers that make no use of that door.

As Jesus pointed out, His people have a spiritual instinct that causes them to know when they are hearing the truth of God and when they aren't (vv. 4-5). But even God's people can be led astray. So we must be on guard. Listening to preachers is no small thing. Our spiritual wellbeing is at stake. So let's listen carefully and careful listening means listening for Christ, who is the door.

I thank God that, in my childhood years, I sat under the preaching of a man who put the door before me. He made me aware of the sinfulness that barred me from heaven, and when I began to feel the despair of being a sinner, my faithful pastor gloriously said: "Jesus is the door to heaven."

I heard that marvelous news and fled to Jesus. When I finally arrive in heaven, I want to find that Christ-preaching pastor, fall on his neck, and kiss him in gratitude for pointing me to the door.

October 10

"I Am the Good Shepherd" (Jesus)

From God's Word, the Bible...

"I am the good shepherd. The good shepherd gives His life for the sheep."
"I am the good shepherd; and I know My sheep, and am known by My own."

John 10:11,14

I need a shepherd. Just as I need a door, so I need a shepherd—a door to give me access to the kingdom of God and eternal life, and a shepherd to feed, guide, and protect me. Jesus is both the door and the shepherd that I need. Shortly after He healed a blind man in Jerusalem, Jesus claimed to be both.

There are false ministers and false ministries that have no door in them. They can't tell people how to enter heaven. And they, like the Pharisees of old, can't really shepherd people. In the previous reading, we looked at Jesus as the door. Now we look at Him as the shepherd.

The Lord Jesus is the good shepherd. No one can compare to Him. He uses ministers to shepherd His flock, but they are only under-shepherds. If they are what they ought to be, they are mindful that the sheep don't belong to them. The sheep belong to Christ, and they are to be shepherded with that in mind. They are to be shepherded in the way that the Lord wants it done.

How is it that the Lord Jesus has people as His sheep? The answer is that He laid down His life for them. John 10 reports Jesus saying four times that He was going to "lay down" His life for His sheep (vv. 11,15,17,18). That's what happened when Jesus was on the cross. He laid down His life for His sheep. His haters thought they were taking His life from Him. They were wrong. He didn't have to be on that cross. He was there because He chose to be. He was there to die for His sheep.

But why was it necessary for Him to die for His sheep? Could He not have had His flock apart from dying? No. His death was absolutely essential. His sheep would have died if He had not died in their stead.

All of us who are now the Lord's sheep used to be part of another flock. We come into this world as part of Satan's flock. Our sin has placed us in his flock. What a flock it is! The devil is the shepherd, and he holds us in his flock with the chain of sin. The only way out of his flock is for sin's penalty to be paid. If that penalty is paid, he has to let us go. And the penalty? It is everlasting separation from God. The only way for us to pay that penalty ourselves is to be eternally separated from God. But, thank God, Jesus came to pay the penalty for His sheep. He came to experience, on the cross, an eternity of separation from God so His sheep could be released from the devil's flock and be in His flock.

The death of Jesus on the cross was substitutionary. He died in the place of His sheep. He received there what they would receive in eternity if He hadn't died in their place.

All those who trust in the Lord Jesus and what He did for them on the cross are now part of His flock. How can we be part of His flock if He died? The glorious answer is that He didn't stay dead. Yes, He died, but He also rose again. Right here in John 10, we have Him predicting His resurrection in these words: ". . . I lay down My life that I may take it again" (v. 17, see also v. 18).

Believers in Christ are the flock of a living shepherd. By His death on their behalf, He broke the chain of sin. By His resurrection from the grave, He proved that His death on the cross was pleasing to God and effective in securing our salvation.

Now it is our pleasure and delight to live each day as sheep in the flock of our living Savior. It is our delight to feed in the green pasture of His Word. It is our delight to walk peacefully along, knowing that we are free from sin's condemnation. It is our joy to know that even when we stray, He will not let us go but will seek us out and restore us (see Psalm 23).

While we weren't there to hear Jesus say: "I am the good shepherd," we rejoice with joy unspeakable in reading those precious words.

October 11

"I Am the Resurrection and the Life" (Jesus)

From God's Word, the Bible...

Jesus said to her, "I am the resurrection and the life. He who believes in Me, though he may die, he shall live. And whoever lives and believes in Me shall never die. Do you believe this?"

John 11:25-26

Siblings Mary, Martha, and Lazarus were dear to Jesus. But suddenly it didn't seem so. Lazarus had gotten sick, and Jesus hadn't come to heal him. Now he was dead—four days dead! The situation seemed to be utterly hopeless.

Mary and Martha were bewildered. Why hadn't Jesus come when they sent for Him? Why did Jesus let their brother die? They didn't know that Jesus had something in mind that would bring great glory to God and great comfort to them.

After Martha expressed her confidence that her brother would rise again "in the resurrection at the last day" (v. 24), Jesus made the fifth of His seven "I am" sayings. He said: "I am the resurrection and the life." With those words, Jesus was essentially saying to Martha: "There's no need to wait for the resurrection at the end of time. I am the resurrection. The resurrection is here now."

And so it was! Jesus stepped up to the tomb of Lazarus and cried out: "Lazarus, come forth!" (v. 43). John, the author of this Gospel, states the result of that cry with marvelous brevity: "And he who had died came out. . ." (v. 44).

Lazarus was raised because Jesus was the resurrection and the life, just as He claimed.

That claim didn't pertain only to Lazarus. It also pertains to all believers in Christ, but—note it well—only to believers. It gives us consolation about death in all of its forms: physical, spiritual, and eternal.

Regarding physical death, Jesus says: "He who believes in Me, though he may die, he shall live" (v. 25).

Jesus raised Lazarus to give us a picture of the resurrection that awaits all believers. Death isn't final for God's people. The same Jesus who raised Lazarus will eventually come again, and when He comes He will raise the bodies of all His people, and refashion those bodies to conform to the resurrection body that He Himself has (Phil. 3:20-21).

Skeptics love to come up with scenarios that seemingly make the resurrection an impossibility. "What about that person who died thousands of years ago and has completely disintegrated? How could there possibly be a resurrection for him or her?" they ask. To that they add this: "What about that person who was blown to bits in war? Surely, there's nothing left to be raised."

Our answer is: "Look at Lazarus. His case seemed to be impossible, yet Jesus raised him."

Jesus' claim to be the resurrection and the life also pertains to the matter of spiritual death. This is our natural state. It means we are dead toward God. It's easy to miss this in Jesus' words, but it's there. In verse 26, He uses this phrase: "whoever lives and believes in Me."

The believer in Christ already has resurrection life. He is even now living in Christ. By the grace of God, he has been resurrected from spiritual death and made alive in Christ (Eph. 2:1,5-7).

That brings us to the third and final form of death—eternal death. Jesus also addressed that in His claim to be the resurrection and the life. He says those who believe in Him "shall never die" (v. 26).

The believer will never be separated from God in the world to come. He will never experience "the second death" (Rev. 20:14-15).

Unbelievers, who are already dead spiritually, have two more deaths to go—physical death and eternal death. With believers in Christ, it's different. Having been rescued from spiritual death, they only have one more death ahead of them. That is physical death, and those who are alive when Jesus comes won't even experience that (1 Thess. 4:17).

What a joy it is to be a Christian! We have already been made alive in Christ. We don't dread physical death because we know it won't be the final word for our bodies. And we never have to worry about eternal death because Christ has given us eternal life.

October 12

"I Am the Way, the Truth, and the Life" (Jesus)

From God's Word, the Bible...

Jesus said to him, "I am the way, the truth, and the life. No one comes to the Father except through Me."

John 14:6

I am not ashamed to say that I want to go to heaven when I die. Nothing is more important to me than that. I am a mortal being passing with blinding speed through this world. Yes, I want to go to heaven!

If I'm to go to heaven, I must have a way. I don't need two, three or four ways. One will do. I won't reject that way merely because it's the only way. If there's only one way, I will rejoice in it and avail myself of it.

What a horrible thing it would be to know that heaven in all its glory is out there, but there's no way to get to it!

We don't have to face that horror because there is a way. The way is Jesus.

It was the night before His crucifixion, and Jesus was alone with His eleven disciples (Judas already having departed). These disciples were filled with sorrow because they now knew full well that Jesus would soon depart from them.

Their sorrow so touched the heart of Jesus that He offered one consolation after another to them. One of those consolations was heaven, which Jesus referred to as His Father's "house" (v. 1).

Furthermore, Jesus assured the disciples that they knew the "where" and the "way" (v. 4). They knew where He was going, and they knew the way to get there. Thomas begged to differ, saying: "Lord, we do not know where You are going, and how can we know the way?" (v. 5).

It was at that point that Jesus gave the sixth of His seven "I am" sayings: "I am the way, the truth, and the life" (v. 6).

Wonderful news! There is a way to get to heaven, and that way is Jesus!

How is it that Jesus is the way to heaven? What is there about Him that makes Him the way? The answer is His death on the cross. Let's never forget that everything we read in John 14 is set in the context of the cross.

What is so special about Jesus' death on the cross? In dying there, Jesus received the penalty for sin. It is our sin that blocks our entrance into heaven. God won't allow sinners to enter there in their sin. Their sin must be removed, and the only way sin can be removed is for its penalty to be paid. Jesus went to the cross to pay that penalty. He went there to receive the wrath of God in the place of sinners. Since Jesus paid the penalty for sin, it can no longer bar us from heaven. By His death on the cross, Jesus took sin out of the way, and He became the way.

It's very important that we understand that Jesus wasn't simply claiming to be a way to heaven. He says He is "the way." Jesus is the only way to heaven because He is the only one who could deal with the sin that keeps us out of heaven.

In addition to claiming to be the way, Jesus claims to be the "the truth and the life." I suggest that those terms are subsidiary to the way. It is "the way" that predominates in this sentence. "The truth" and "the life" are themselves part of Jesus being the way.

What does it mean for Jesus to be the truth? It means that He reveals to us every truth that pertains to salvation. He shows us the sin that keeps us from heaven, and the cross that removes the sin.

What does it mean for Jesus to be the life? The Bible tells us that we are "dead in trespasses and sins" (Eph. 2:1). It doesn't help a dead person to have a way to heaven put before him. He can't walk it. When Jesus called Himself "the life," He was affirming that He not only shows sinners the way to heaven but also gives them the ability to walk that way.

All of salvation is God's grace. It is God's grace that there is a way to heaven. It is God's grace that shows us the way. And it is God's grace that enables us to walk the way. So, to say it again, the way is Jesus.

What a cheering word this was for the eleven disciples who heard it on the night before the Lord Jesus was crucified! It is no less cheering as we read today what He said then. Are you trusting in Christ as the Way to heaven, and are you on your way there?

October 13

"I Am the Vine" (Jesus)

FROM GOD'S WORD, THE BIBLE...

"I am the true vine, and My Father is the vinedresser."
"I am the vine, you are the branches. He who abides in Me, and I in him, bears much fruit; for without Me you can do nothing."

JOHN 15:1, 5

God made us to bear fruit for Him. How do we live up to that purpose? How do we bear fruit for God? We do so by obeying His commandments. In keeping those commandments, we reflect His image and we bring honor to His name.

Sin makes us unfruitful. It causes us to come short of the purpose for which God made us. Sin is refusing to obey God's commandments. Every time we refuse to obey, we fail to reflect God's image and to live for His glory. We might say sin makes all of us unfruitful vines.

God could have given up on us. He could have said: "I will never get any fruit from those sinful people." He could have just plowed us under.

But God took another approach. He sent His Son, Jesus, to be "the true vine" (v. 1). We are all dead vines, bearing no fruit for God because of our sin. But all is not lost. We can still bear fruit for God, not as vines in and of ourselves, but by being connected to the Lord Jesus, who is the true vine. If we abide in Jesus, we shall bear "much fruit" (v. 5).

By calling Himself the "true vine," Jesus was affirming that He is the only vine that works in this matter of bearing fruit for God. Merely belonging to a church won't work. That is a false vine. Performing a few good works here and there won't work. That is another false vine. No one will ever be able to produce the fruit that God demands and finally enter into heaven, except through the Lord Jesus Christ. Apart from Him, we can do nothing (v. 5).

So, the most urgent matter in this life is to make sure we are connected to the vine, that is, to make sure we are connected to Christ. This takes place by God graciously working in us and bringing us to faith. By grace through faith we are saved (Eph. 2:8-9).

Jesus mentions a dreadful possibility in regard to the issue of being connected with Him. It is having the appearance of being connected without actually being connected (v. 6). Judas Iscariot would be the prime example of this. Everyone would have said that he was truly connected to Christ, but he wasn't.

Look at what happens to those who aren't truly in Christ. They are taken away (v. 2), "cast out" (v. 6), "withered" (v. 6) and "burned" (v. 6).

How few these days seems to realize the tremendous weight of these words! Let's make sure we allow them to sink in. A great day of taking away is coming for all those who aren't in Christ (Matt. 7:21-23).

How do we know that we are truly connected to Christ? We must ask ourselves two questions. The first is this: Am I producing fruit? Am I obeying the Lord's commandments and living for His glory? Those who don't produce fruit, no matter what they profess, aren't vitally connected to the vine, which is Jesus.

All Christians produce fruit, but not all are equally fruitful. We've all noticed this. Some Christians grow robust and strong, while others are stunted. The Lord wants all of us to reach the level of "much fruit." To achieve that end, He resorts to that measure all gardeners are familiar with—pruning. One of His sharp pruning devices is His Word. He uses it to cut away things that are hindering our spiritual growth and productivity (Heb. 4:12). God may also use chastisement to the same end.

God's pruning devices can be painful, but they produce positive results. They yield the positive fruit of righteousness, and they prove to us that we are indeed connected to Christ (Heb. 12:3-11).

The second question we must ask ourselves is this: Am I abiding in Christ? To abide in the Lord means we continue with Him. We continue believing, obeying, and serving. Continuance—endurance—is ever the mark of reality (John 8:31; 1 John 2:24; 2 John 9). If we don't continue in the faith, it's because we never really possessed it (1 John 2:19).

God says to me: "You are a worthless, fruitless, dead vine, but I am going to get fruit from you by connecting you to a living, fruitful vine." I think I would like to have been there to hear Jesus say: "I am the vine."

October 14

Jesus Speaks to His Father

From God's Word, the Bible...

Jesus spoke these words, lifted up His eyes to heaven, and said: "Father, the hour has come. Glorify Your Son, that Your Son also may glorify You. . . ."

John 17:1

The seventeenth chapter of John records a prayer that Jesus prayed the night before He was crucified. This wasn't the prayer that He offered in Gethsemane. The opening words of John 18 indicate that Jesus prayed this prayer while He and His eleven true disciples were still in the Upper Room. So all of those disciples heard the prayer. Jesus had given them many words of comfort and encouragement prior to this prayer, but they probably found it to be more comforting than anything else He said.

These men had heard Jesus preach and teach on many occasions. Blessed men were they! On this night they were privileged to hear Him offer the most wonderful prayer ever prayed. I'm sure these disciples had heard Jesus pray on numerous occasions, but this prayer—there was none like it!

The prayer falls into three easily discernible parts. First, *Jesus prayed that His Father would be glorified* (vv. 1-5).

At first glance, it doesn't seem so because Jesus begins: "Father, the hour has come. Glorify Your Son. . ." (v. 1).

The reason Jesus began that way quickly becomes apparent. It was necessary for Jesus to be glorified so He could glorify the Father.

The word "glorify" means "to honor" or "to magnify." The consuming priority of Jesus' life was to bring honor to His Father (John 7:18; 8:50; 12:27-28; 13:31-32).

To honor His Father meant that Jesus would have to finish the work the Father had sent Him to do. That was the work of the cross by which He would secure the gift of eternal life for all those who were "given" to Him by the Father (v. 2). Before the world began, the Father gave Jesus to us, and He gave all believers to the Lord Jesus. What a wonderful double gift!

Let's not miss this important detail in this part of Jesus' prayer—He speaks of the work on the cross as being already finished (v. 4). He is yet to be crucified, but He speaks as if He had already been crucified. This shows us that there was no uncertainty about whether Jesus would complete the work of redemption.

Jesus also prayed for the eleven disciples who were with Him (vv. 6-19). He prayed that they be kept or protected (vv.11,15), that they be united (v.11), that they experience His joy (v.13), and that they be sanctified or separated from the world (v.17).

His disciples would need protection because the world would hate them (v. 14). There's no surprise here because the hating world is under the control of "the evil one" (v.15).

Jesus may have prayed for His disciples to be united for this very reason—the evil one who inspires the hatred of the world works feverishly to alienate believers from each other. And He may have prayed for them to know His joy to sustain them in a world that could wring the joy out of them.

His disciples would need to be sanctified or set apart because this evil world carries a strange attraction for believers and has the power to draw them away from faithfulness to Christ. If believers are to maintain purity in such a world, they must immerse themselves in "the truth" (v.19), that is, the Word of God.

Finally, *Jesus prayed for His future disciples* (vv. 20-24). He first asked that they also be united (v. 21). We shouldn't think He was speaking in terms of mere organizational unity. It was spiritual unity that He had in mind. We know all too well that people who belong to one church don't necessarily have unity. On the other hand, Christians who belong to different denominations don't necessarily find themselves divided. There is a kinship among all true Christians, regardless of their denominational distinctions.

Jesus also prayed that His future disciples would share His glory. This petition will finally be fulfilled when we get to heaven.

Jesus concluded his prayer by resolving to declare the Father's name (vv. 25-26). He had, of course, declared it to the disciples during His time with them, and He was determined to continue to declare it. By His death on the cross, His resurrection, His post-resurrection appearances, His ascension, and His gift of the Holy Spirit to his church, the Lord Jesus abundantly kept this resolve.

The eleven men who heard that prayer had to know that they were listening to words "fitly spoken" and must have rejoiced in having such a Savior.

October 15

"Father, Forgive Them. . ." (Jesus)

From God's Word, the Bible...

Then Jesus said, "Father, forgive them,
for they do not know what they do."
And they divided His garments and cast lots.

Luke 23:34

The first words from Jesus' lips after He was nailed to cross were these: "Father, forgive them, for they do not know what they do."

I know I shouldn't be surprised to read that Jesus' first words from the cross came in the form of a prayer. Jesus was a man of prayer, and Luke loved to emphasize this. He informs us that Jesus prayed at His baptism (3:21), before selecting His disciples (6:12), on the Mount of Transfiguration (9:28-29), and on the night before He was crucified (22:41,44). Luke also tells us that Jesus "often withdrew into the wilderness and prayed" (5:16). In addition to praying Himself, Jesus taught His disciples that "men always ought to pray and not lose heart" (18:1).

But I'm still somewhat surprised to read that Jesus prayed. I think my surprise is due to Luke writing the word "Then." "Then Jesus said, 'Father, forgive them. . . .'"

There's a ton of marvel in that "Then." By using it Luke is reminding us of all that had happened to Jesus in the hours preceding His crucifixion. Taken into custody in the middle of the night to endure legal proceedings that were themselves illegal! Mocked, ridiculed and spat on! Scourged until the flesh of His back was a mass of bloody ribbons! Crowned with a crown of thorns! Paraded through the streets of Jerusalem and out to Golgotha! Nailed to the cross! Think about all of it, and then think about it again, and then marvel at Luke's "Then." It captures all of these things. After all the humiliation, the pain, and the ridicule, Jesus prays!

Part of the marvel of Luke's "Then" is that Jesus addresses God as "Father." Although His Father could have saved Him from the cross, the Lord Jesus isn't angry. There's love and trust in His word, "Father." We need to learn from Jesus to continue to love and trust God when our circumstances rise up against us, saying with Edward Mote:

When darkness seems to hide His face,
I rest on His unchanging grace.
When all around my soul gives way
He then is all my hope and stay.

But now we move from "Then" to "them." Jesus prays: "Father, forgive them. . . ." In the midst of His excruciating pain, Jesus is thinking about His Father and about others. He had taught that love for God and love for others are the greatest of the commandments, and He is practicing those commandments even as He dies.

But for whom is He praying when He uses the word "them?" The Jewish leaders who were behind His crucifixion? The Roman soldiers who nailed Him to the cross? The multitude that stood staring at Him?

Charles Spurgeon says:

> I love this prayer . . . because of the indistinctness of it. . . . Now into that pronoun "them" I feel that I can crawl. Can you get in there? Oh, by a humble faith appropriate the cross of Christ by trusting in it: and get into that big little word "them"! It seems like a chariot of mercy that has come down to earth, into which a man may step and it shall bear him up to heaven.[2]

A young fellow who was angry with his mother included in his bedtime prayer a reference to everyone in the family except her. When he crawled into bed, he looked at her and said: "I suppose you noticed you were not in it."

How very thankful we should be, as Spurgeon pointed out, that there's room in Jesus' "them" for all who want God's forgiveness! Let's not debate the word "them," but rather do as Spurgeon urged and "crawl" in there.

Jesus' prayer from the cross is an apple of gold. Have you seen the marvel of it? Avis B. Christiansen saw it and wrote:

"Father, forgive them!" thus did He pray,
E'en while His life blood flowed fast away;
Praying for sinners while in such woe—
No one but Jesus ever loved so.

Blessed Redeemer! Precious Redeemer!
Seems now I see Him on Calvary's tree;
Wounded and bleeding, for sinners pleading,
Blind and unheeding—dying for me!

2 Charles Spurgeon, *Metropolitan Tabernacle Pulpit*, Pilgrim Publications, Pasadena, TX, no date, vol. 38, p. 318.

"Today, You Will Be with Me in Paradise" (Jesus)

From God's Word, the Bible...

And Jesus said to him, "Assuredly, I say to you, today you will be with Me in Paradise."

Luke 23:43

The Lord Jesus was hanging on a cross between two common criminals, and the religious leaders of the Jews were filled with glee. To them it was the ultimate proof that He was a fraud. He wouldn't have been there between two thieves if He really was the Messiah. Little did they realize that what they regarded as proof of their position was just the opposite. The prophet Isaiah had said that in His death the Messiah would be "numbered with the transgressors" (Isa. 53:12).

One of these two thieves, after initially joining in the mockery that was being heaped on Jesus, suddenly stopped and said to Him: "Lord, remember me when You come into Your kingdom."

Jesus answered that prayer by assuring the man that the two of them would be together that day in Paradise. So the first time Jesus spoke from the cross was to pray. The second time He spoke was to answer prayer.

Let's think about this thief: he was, by his own admission, a sinful man (v. 41). The Lord Jesus was dying the death of a criminal, but He was innocent. This man was dying the death of a criminal because he was a criminal.

To state the obvious, this thief was also a dying man. His wasted life was quickly drawing to a close. His blood was flowing out of his tortured body and falling to the ground. Hell's mouth was opening wide to receive his soul.

Sinful and dying! That sounds just like us! We are all sinners, and we are all dying. It's important for us to identify with this thief because it is only as we do that we are in the position to receive the thrilling assurances that he received.

What were those assurances? One was that he, the thief, was right about Jesus. He called Him "Lord," and Jesus didn't correct or rebuke him. Jesus accepted the title and responded to this man in the fashion of being Lord. It was God's grace that enabled this man to see the truth about Jesus because "no one can say that Jesus is Lord except by the Holy Spirit" (1 Cor. 12:3).

Another assurance that the thief received was that he was right to believe in heaven. Jesus didn't say to him: "You're wrong about this business of Me coming into My kingdom. There's no such place as heaven. You might as well accept the fact that when people die, they're dead. That's all there is to it."

The truth is that heaven is a present reality for those who believe in Christ. The Lord Jesus said, "Today," to this man. That means that his soul would go to heaven as soon as he died. The Apostle Paul assures us that as soon as we are absent from the body, we are present with the Lord (2 Cor. 5:6-8).

Yet another assurance was that Jesus does indeed possess the authority to open heaven's door. Jesus didn't say to him: "You're talking to the wrong person. I'm not the way to heaven." Instead He promised that this man would enter heaven that very day.

This thief had been wrong all of his life, but suddenly "the wrong man" had become "the right man." He came to the right person, Jesus, about the right matter, heaven, and he came in the right way, humbly casting himself on the Lord for mercy.

The words of Jesus to this dying thief were an apple of gold. Fitly spoken words were they! How thankful we should be that they are reported to us in Scripture! They assure us that we will have a home in heaven if we will come to Jesus. No matter how sinful we have been, we can be forgiven.

But we must never think of this one thief without thinking of the other. This man refused to cast himself upon the mercy of the Lord. So he died without salvation, and without salvation he couldn't enter heaven. It wasn't an accident that Jesus' cross was placed between these two thieves. He is the great divider of men. Those who receive Him are saved. Those who reject Him are lost. On which side of the Lord Jesus are you?

October 17

"Woman, Behold Your Son" (Jesus)

FROM GOD'S WORD, THE BIBLE...

When Jesus therefore saw His mother, and the disciple whom He loved standing by, He said to His mother, "Woman, behold your son!" Then He said to the disciple, "Behold your mother!" And from that hour that disciple took her to his own home.

JOHN 19:26-27

All of Jesus' disciples had fled from Him in the hours preceding His crucifixion, but John, the author of this Gospel, had thought better of his cowardice, and had taken his place at the foot of Jesus' cross. We know he was there because he identifies himself as "the disciple whom Jesus loved."

By using that title for himself, John was able to avoid using his name again and again in this Gospel. It was his way of being modest. But it was also more than that. The glory of John's life lay in knowing that he was loved by the Lord Jesus. John didn't glory in his love for Christ. It was far too weak and faltering for that. But the love of the Lord for him, ah, that was something in which to glory. Reflecting on that love must have been the thing that drew him back to his rightful place.

John wasn't alone at the foot of the cross. Jesus' mother, Mary, was there with him, and Jesus, in the anguish of suffering, could see them there. That prompted Him to speak His third word from the cross. A double word it was—spoken first to Mary and then to John. "Woman, behold your son!" and then, "Behold your mother!"

Jesus' meaning was clear. He was committing the care of His mother to John. In doing so, He was manifesting tender concern for one who was in great need. The future must have looked very bleak to Mary. What was to become of her? Jesus' words gave the answer, and those words found their mark because we read that John "from that hour" took Mary "to his own home" (v. 27).

So, Jesus wasn't so occupied with His own needs that He neglected the needs of His mother. Others had always been at the forefront of Jesus' life, and they were again in His death. His first three words from the cross were spoken on behalf of others. This isn't surprising. His first priority was God; His second was others.

The Lord Jesus is still concerned about the needs of others today. So we can and should bring our needs to Him. In heaven as our High Priest, He sympathizes with us in all of our cares (Heb. 4:15).

And Jesus' concern for others teaches us who follow Him to be concerned about others as well. Have we learned this lesson, or have we fallen prey to the self-centeredness that is so prevalent these days?

In committing His mother to John's care, Jesus was showing His concern for what was left of her life in this world. But He didn't allow that issue, important as it was, to crowd out a larger issue—the life beyond this world.

This comes out in a couple of ways. First, the fact that Jesus was concerned about Mary and her physical needs didn't bring Him down from the cross. He didn't have to stay on the cross. He could have laid aside the work He was doing there. He could have put Mary's physical needs above the work of redemption, but He didn't. He gave priority to the matter of opening the door of heaven to all who savingly believe in Him.

Many seem to only be interested in the Jesus of physical needs, wanting Him to be exclusively concerned about them in the here and now. They want to accept the lesser gift of His care for the problems of this life, while they reject the greater gift of eternal life. The tragedy is that they can have both.

The second indication that Jesus gave priority to the next life is shown in the way that He addressed Mary. He called her "Woman." Some are disturbed by this because they think Jesus was being rude to His mother. Nothing could be farther from the truth. Jesus addressed Mary as "Woman," not to be rude, but rather to underscore a most vital truth, namely, that their relationship was now forever changed. Mary was now a simple believer in her Lord—the One who had purchased her salvation by dying on the cross.

Jesus created a new family with His words to Mary and John. Through His death, Jesus creates a new family for all those who believe—the family of God. What a blessing that is!

October 18

"My God, My God, Why Have You Forsaken Me?" (Jesus)

From God's Word, the Bible...

Now from the sixth hour until the ninth hour there was darkness over all the land. And about the ninth hour Jesus cried out with a loud voice, saying, "Eli, Eli, lama sabachthani?" that is, "My God, My God, why have You forsaken Me?"

Matthew 27:45-46

Jesus was nailed to the cross at nine in the morning. He died at three in the afternoon. The first three of His seven words from the cross were spoken during His first three hours on the cross. The last four were spoken in quick succession just before He died.

From noon to three, Jesus said nothing. These were the hours when darkness fell over the land, the hours at which the sun normally shines most brightly. After those three long hours, Jesus cried: "My God, My God, why have You forsaken Me?"

This was His fourth word, with three on each side of it. It was the center word. That is strikingly appropriate because it brings us to the very center of the meaning of Jesus' death. It is Jesus' own explanation of those hours of darkness. They were hours in which God withdrew from Him.

Why did the Father withdraw from Jesus? If we are to understand this amazing thing, we must address the problem the cross was designed to deal with—the problem created by man's sinfulness and God's holiness.

What is sin? It is refusing to live according to God's commandments. God cannot and will not regard sin as a trifling matter. Why does God take sin so seriously? He is holy, and His holy nature requires Him to judge sin. For God to ignore sin or refuse to punish it would make Him guilty of sin Himself.

But it's not enough to say God is holy. He is. But He is also gracious. And while His holiness demands that He judge sinners by forever separating them from Himself, His grace demands that He forgive sinners.

How could the holy God both punish sinners and let them go free? How could He both satisfy the demands of His justice and the demands of His grace when those demands seemed to be conflicting and contradictory? The answer is the cross of Christ. The Apostle Paul says that Jesus was "made" sin on the cross (2 Cor. 5:21). The sins of others were laid on Him.

For God to count Jesus as guilty of the sins of others required Him, God, to forsake Jesus because the penalty for sin is God-forsakenness (2 Thess. 1:9). If God had refused to truly forsake Jesus, He could not have counted Him the substitute for sinners. That forsaking had to take place!

Some people argue that God did not really forsake Jesus on the cross. It was rather a matter of Jesus only feeling that He was forsaken. But if that had not been a true forsaking, there would have been no atonement for sinners.

The glory of it all is that God only requires that the penalty for sin be paid once. If Jesus paid it, there is no penalty left for all those who take refuge in Jesus through faith. In other words, God cannot punish Jesus for my sins and then proceed to punish me as well. That would be unjust! If Jesus bore my God-forsakenness on the cross, there is, therefore, no such forsakenness for me to bear. The cross was, then, God's way of satisfying both the demands of His justice and His grace. Justice looked upon the cross that day and said: "I'm satisfied. The penalty of God-forsakenness against sinners has been carried out."

And grace looked upon that same cross and said: "I'm satisfied. Since Jesus bore the penalty of God-forsakenness for all who believe, they will never have to bear it themselves and can, therefore, be forgiven."

If someone asks how Jesus could bear in a short period of time an eternity's worth of wrath, we must admit that we are out of our element. We can only say that as God in human flesh, Jesus had the capacity to bear an infinite measure of wrath in a finite length of time.

God will either find our sins on Jesus or on us. If He finds them on Jesus, we will never have to endure their penalty, but if He finds them on us, we must hear from God those tragic words: "Depart from Me" (Matt. 7:23; 25:41).

We can read Jesus' cry to the Father and say: "Jesus forsaken by His Father! What a horrible thing!" Yes, it was. But we can also read those same words and say: "In that cry lies my salvation! What a wonderful thing!"

October 19

"I Thirst" (Jesus)

From God's Word, the Bible...

After this, Jesus, knowing that all things were now accomplished, that the Scripture might be fulfilled, said, "I thirst!" Now a vessel full of sour wine was sitting there; and they filled a sponge with sour wine, put it on hyssop, and put it to His mouth.

John 19:28-29

We have no trouble seeing the significance of the first four statements that Jesus made from the cross. But this statement! What are we to make of it?

It's no surprise that Jesus was thirsty. Many hours had probably elapsed without Him having taken a sip of water. The question is rather why John thought it important to report this cry. There would seem to be no great significance in a dying man thirsting and asking for a drink.

The answer, I think, is that John, prompted by the Holy Spirit, saw truths of great importance in Jesus' thirst. He, John, understood that there was more to Jesus' thirst than mere thirst. There was more to it than what lies on the surface. John wanted us to know about Jesus' thirst so we would know the truth about Jesus. And what is that truth? It is that Jesus was fully God and fully man.

Why is this important? Why do we need to know that Jesus was the God-man? We need to understand that Jesus came to this earth and went to that cross to serve as the mediator between God and sinful men and women. A mediator is one who steps between parties in conflict and makes peace between them.

For Jesus to be the mediator between God and people, He had to represent each. To represent God, He had to be God. There was no problem there. He was already God. He had always been God. But He also had to represent men. To do that, He had to do that which we celebrate at Christmas—He had to take our humanity. That doesn't mean that He laid aside His deity. It rather means that He added our humanity to His deity. In doing that, He became the God-man and was able to represent both God and men.

Let's get back to the matter of Jesus' thirst. How did it show that Jesus was God? The answer is that it was a fulfillment of prophecy (Ps. 69:21).

We must not think that Jesus was a mere helpless victim when He died on the cross. We can go so far as to say that Jesus was in control of His own crucifixion. He was keeping a mental checklist of all the prophecies that His crucifixion had to fulfill, and crying "I thirst" was one of them.

Very few realize the immense importance of Jesus fulfilling prophecies. One author calculated the probability of one man fulfilling forty-eight prophecies of the Old Testament to a blindfolded man picking a marked electron out of a one-inch line of electrons. It would take nineteen million years just to count those electrons! Supposing the blindfolded man could actually pick up an electron, what chance would he have of getting the one that was marked? It's the same probability of one man fulfilling forty-eight Old Testament prophecies. And Jesus fulfilled, not 48, but 325!

Yes, the thirst of Jesus shows us that He was God, but it also shows us that He was fully man. "I thirst," is a human cry. Thirst means we have a need, and God doesn't need anything. God doesn't get thirsty.

The thirst of Jesus, if we will let it, will convince us that Jesus' humanity was real. It will persuade us to not downplay His humanity. Some have a tendency to do this. They seem to think that it is a disservice to Jesus to emphasize His humanity. They give the impression that Jesus' humanity was only a pretend humanity.

We must never minimize the humanity of Christ for this reason—there would be no salvation without it. It was humanity that sinned against God, and God's justice demanded that humanity pay the penalty for sin. For Jesus to pay that penalty on our behalf, He had to be one of us.

The thirst of Jesus takes us to the very heart of our salvation because it takes us to the true identity of the One who came to provide that salvation. Jesus thirsted on the cross as the God-man so we could both thirst for salvation and have that thirst quenched:

I heard the voice of Jesus say,
"Behold, I freely give
The living water; thirsty one,
stoop down and drink, and live"
I came to Jesus, and I drank
Of that life-giving stream;
My thirst was quenched, my soul revived,
And now I live in Him.
(Horatius Bonar)

October 20

"It Is Finished!" (Jesus)

From God's Word, the Bible...

So when Jesus had received the sour wine, He said, "It is finished!" And bowing His head, He gave up His spirit.

John 19:30

It's easy to think of lots of things that we are glad to have out of the way. Boring meetings, car trouble, sickness and socializing with difficult, obnoxious people—all fall into that category. When we come to the end of such things, we might well exclaim, "I'm glad that's over!"

We might think that the sixth word Jesus spoke from the cross belongs in the category of rejoicing to have reached the end of something unpleasant. Crucifixion was such an incredibly horrid and agonizing thing, we can well imagine crucified men finally gasping: "It's finally over!"

But that's not what Jesus was saying when He cried, "It is finished!" He wasn't speaking as a tortured man who was glad to see His suffering come to an end. There's a huge difference between ending something and accomplishing something. With His cry, Jesus wasn't merely saying that He was ending something. He was saying that He had accomplished something.

What is the "it" to which Jesus referred? It was the "it" which brought Him to this world. What was that "it"? Jesus Himself stated it several times. In Luke 19:10, we find Him saying: "The Son of Man has come to seek and to save that which was lost."

In Mark 10:45, He says: ". . . the Son of Man did not come to be served but to serve, and to give His life a ransom for many."

In John 3:17, He says: "For God did not send His Son into the world to condemn the world, but that the world through Him might be saved."

These are just three of the many verses in which Jesus talks about the "it" that brought Him to earth. These verses tell us that Jesus came to provide salvation for sinners, and that He had to die in their stead in order to provide it.

The "it" to which Jesus was referring when He died was the "it" of our salvation. As we noted in a previous reading, "it" is the "it" of Psalm 40:7 (and Hebrews 10:7) when Jesus said to God the Father:

"Behold, I come;
In the scroll of the Book, it is written of me."

Do you see the "it" in those words? When Jesus came to this earth, He told the Father that He was coming to do the "it" that He and the Father had planned before the world began—the salvation for sinners. With the cry, "It is finished!" Jesus was affirming that He had accomplished that which He, the Father, and the Holy Spirit had planned. He wasn't speaking as a victim, but rather as a victor who had crossed the finish line.

What did finishing this "it" require of Jesus? In other words, what exactly did Jesus have to do to accomplish our salvation? What was necessary to save sinners from sin?

First, Jesus had to live a sinless life, that is, a life of perfect obedience to God. This was God's requirement from the very beginning. If Adam and Eve had perfectly obeyed the commandment God gave them in Eden, they would have received the gift of eternal life. God has never changed the condition for receiving that life. He still demands perfect obedience from us. We can't meet this demand, but Jesus met it. He lived the sinless life that God requires, and God puts the righteousness of Christ to the account of all who come to Christ. He counts Christ's righteousness as though it were their righteousness.

But what about our sins? Jesus went to the cross, not to die as others do, but rather to die a special death. He went there to receive the wrath that our sins deserve.

Here is Christianity in a nutshell: Jesus got my sins on the cross, and I get His righteousness.

When Jesus cried, "It is finished!" He was affirming that He had completed the work of salvation for all who would believe in Him. He had met all the requirements for saving sinners.

Perhaps someone will ask about the resurrection of Jesus. Why did Jesus claim that everything was finished before His resurrection? The answer is that He had done all that He came to do. It was the Father's work to raise Him from the dead (Acts 2:42; 17:31).

We should rejoice over Jesus' cry. We couldn't be saved without it. It is an apple of gold in a setting of silver.

October 21

"Father, into Your Hands, I Commit My Spirit" (Jesus)

From God's Word, the Bible...

And when Jesus had cried out with a loud voice, He said, "Father, 'into Your hands I commit My spirit.'" Having said this, He breathed His last.

Luke 23:46

The last words spoken from the cross reveal that Jesus died with great confidence and without fear and trembling. He spoke of death in terms of placing Himself in His Father's hands. His words draw the picture of someone depositing something for safe keeping with one who is unquestionably trustworthy.

Would we know how to die? We should look to the Lord Jesus. His last words from the cross show us that *we can die well if we die knowing God is our heavenly Father.*

Of course, we can't have God as our Father in exactly the same way that Jesus did. Jesus was—and is—the eternal Son of God. But we can still have God as our Father. This is the glory of the Christian message. Each of us can know God through the redeeming work of Christ.

Some argue that God is already the Father of all, but a quick glance at Scripture reveals that this is not true. In John 1:12, we read of Jesus: "But as many as received Him, to them He gave the right to become children of God, even those who believe in His name."

Who can be called the children of God? Is it everyone without exception? No. This verse says that only those who believe in Christ are the children of God. Those who reject Christ don't have God as their Father (John 8:42).

We also learn from Jesus' last words that *we can die well if we die knowing that our souls will go immediately into the hands of our heavenly Father.*

Jesus had been in the hands of wicked people (Matt. 17:22-23; 26:45). As He died, He knew that was no longer the case. Human hands had done all that they could do to Him, and now He could commit Himself into His Father's hands.

Jesus knew His soul was going to be received by the Father at the very moment of His death. His body, of course, would be placed in a tomb and would be resurrected on the third day. At the time of His resurrection, His soul and body would be reunited. But His soul was safe in the Father's hands while His body was entombed.

It's exactly the same with each person who knows God. At the point of death, his soul goes immediately into God's presence and remains there until his body is raised from the grave. At that time, his soul and body will be joined together again and will live forever with the Lord (1 Thess. 4:13-18).

For the Christian, this takes the sting out of death. Tell him that he is about to die, and he will rejoice in knowing that to be absent from the body is to be present with the Lord (2 Cor. 5:6-8). The unbeliever doesn't have this comfort. There's another set of hands ready to receive him at the moment of death.

We should also learn from Jesus' dying words that *we can die well if we die knowing our work is done.*

Jesus spoke His last word from the cross immediately after He cried: "It is finished!" The Lord Jesus came into this world with a mission that was clearly laid out for Him by His Father. Jesus carefully and diligently followed that plan. He was able to say: "For I have come down from heaven, not to do My own will, but the will of Him who sent Me" (John 6:38).

God also has a plan for all those who belong to Christ. He has given them a work to do even as He gave Jesus work to do. We are called to "proclaim the praises" of God who has called us "out of darkness into His marvelous light" (1 Peter 2:9). We're to be fulfilling this purpose in our families, on our jobs and in our churches and communities. Wherever we go and whatever we do, we are to be conscious that we belong to God and that we are to live for God.

Because we are fallible and frail, we cannot perfectly fulfill our purpose as the Lord Jesus did His, but we can be striving to do better all the time, knowing as we strive that death will be far more comfortable for those that so strive.

Jesus' dying word was a fitly spoken word. We should make Him our example by seeking to live as He lived and to die as He died.

October 22

A Centurion Speaks about Jesus

From God's Word, the Bible...

So when the centurion and those with him, who were guarding Jesus, saw the earthquake and the things that had happened, they feared greatly, saying, "Truly this was the Son of God!"

Matthew 27:54

The Gospels report several impressive confessions of faith. There's one from John the Baptist (John 1:29) and one from Nathanael (John 1:49). There are two from Simon Peter (Matt. 16:16; John 6:68-69). To these we can add the confessions of all Jesus' disciples (Matt. 14:33), that of Martha (John 11:27), and that of Thomas (John 20:28).

I think that the most impressive of all the confessions presented in the Gospels came from a man who stood at the foot of Jesus' cross. I'm referring to the Roman centurion.

He certainly doesn't qualify as one from whom we would expect an awe-struck confession of faith in Jesus. It's probably safe to assume that this man had supervised many crucifixions. If so, he would have been a very hardened man. Furthermore, since the Romans employed crucifixion for very bad men, this centurion wouldn't have been inclined to conclude that one of them was the Son of God. But that's exactly what he concluded about Jesus.

How long had this man been in direct contact with Jesus? We can't say. It's likely that he was present when the soldiers in his command mocked and scourged Jesus. It's likely that he saw them press their cruel crown of thorns upon His head. He was certainly present when his soldiers prodded Jesus through the streets of Jerusalem and out to Golgotha. He stood watching as his men nailed Jesus to the cross, hoisted it in the air, and dropped it in the ground. He heard the insults and ridicule that were heaped on Jesus by his own soldiers, the religious leaders of the Jews, the two men who were crucified with Jesus, and those who were only passing by. He may have even participated in the mockery himself.

The Bible doesn't tell us that this man made his confession before Jesus was crucified or while He was being crucified. His confession came when Jesus was dead. So, the centurion had to see evidence along the way that Jesus was far more than an ordinary man.

The way Jesus suffered must have made an impression on him. It was obvious that Jesus was different from other men.

And the first words Jesus spoke from the cross asked God to forgive those who were crucifying Him (Luke 23:34). The centurion had never heard anything like that. The men he had seen crucified usually cursed those who were crucifying them.

Jesus said to one of the two thieves who were being crucified with Him: "Assuredly, I say to you, today you will be with Me in Paradise" (Luke 23:43). The centurion must have heard that and asked himself: "Who is this that expresses concern for another while He is enduring such agony? And how can He assure a thief that he will go to heaven?"

The evidence for Jesus was piling up for this centurion, but there was more to come. Darkness fell across the land at the sixth hour. That was noon in Jewish time-keeping. That darkness didn't last for only a few minutes; it lasted for three hours and only began to go away brief moments before Jesus died. The centurion had seen darkness, but he had never seen darkness like this. This was the darkest of all darknesses. In the words of William Hendriksen, it was "intense and unforgettable."

And then there was the earthquake that occurred at the very moment that Jesus died (v. 54). All that the centurion had seen and heard converged upon him in a powerful way. Jesus wasn't just another man dying another death. He was the God-man. The centurion wasn't alone in drawing this conclusion; his soldiers drew it as well.

Some say we shouldn't make too much of what this centurion said. They contend that he was only acknowledging that Jesus was a special man.

I don't doubt for a moment that his confession came from a heart that had been touched and transformed by the grace of God. It makes sense to me that Jesus' death would immediately achieve the end for which it was intended, that is, salvation for both Jews and Gentiles. The former is pictured for us by the saved thief and the latter by the centurion.

Yes, I'm sure this centurion came to real faith in Christ, and I'm also sure that his confession is here to make all of us ask ourselves if we have also come to real faith in the Lord Jesus. Have you come to Him as the Son of God, your Savior and Lord, in repentance and faith?

October 23

"He Is Not Here" (An Angel)

From God's Word, the Bible...

But the angel answered and said to the women, "Do not be afraid, for I know that you seek Jesus who was crucified. He is not here; for He is risen, as He said. Come, see the place where the Lord lay."

Matthew 28:5-6

If a fitly spoken word is an apple of gold in a setting of silver, we have from an angel one of the greatest of all such apples. These words were spoken on the first day of a new week.

The week preceding it had taken the followers of Jesus from "Hallelujah" to horror. The "Hallelujah" part came when Jesus triumphantly rode into Jerusalem. The horror part came when He was arrested, scourged, ridiculed, and crucified.

This new week had to be better even though it was beginning in a sad way with some women making their way to Jesus' tomb with various spices to further anoint His body (Mark 16:1; Luke 24:1).

Their sadness was mingled with anxiety about the huge stone that had been used to seal Jesus' tomb (Mark 16:3). How would they ever manage to roll it away so they could gain access to the body?

Their sadness and anxiety would soon vanish—the anxiety when they saw the stone had been rolled away; the sadness when they realized that there was no dead body to anoint.

They didn't immediately connect the moved stone with Jesus' resurrection. An angel was there at the tomb to make the connection for them, and he did so in these plain and powerful words: "He is not here; for He is risen, as He said" (Matt. 27:6).

The angels of heaven were associated with all of the great redemptive events. An angel announced Jesus' birth to Joseph (Matt. 1:20-25). Gabriel announced Jesus' birth to Mary (Luke 1:26-38). When Jesus was born, a single angel appeared to make the announcement to shepherds outside Bethlehem (Luke 2:11). After the announcement was made, the one angel was joined by "a multitude of the heavenly host praising God" (Luke 2:13). Angels "came and ministered" to Jesus after He was tempted by Satan in the wilderness (Matt. 4:11). In the midst of Jesus' agony in Gethsemane, an angel "appeared to Him from heaven, strengthening Him" (Luke 22:43).

The angels of heaven must have hovered near as the events in Gethsemane and on Golgotha unfolded because Jesus said He could at any moment call twelve legions of them (Matt. 26:53). And the angels would be present when the Lord Jesus ascended to heaven (Acts 1:10-11). So, it is certainly no surprise to find angels present at Jesus' resurrection.

The fact that the angels were present at every point along redemption's road speaks volumes about the nature of redemption. Angels are glorious, magnificent beings. If the work of redemption required their presence all along the way, it must also be glorious and magnificent. Do we see the glory of redemption? The angels are so fascinated by the redemption of sinners that they desire to look into it (1 Peter 2:12). Does God's work of saving sinners fascinate us?

There was a bit of rebuke and a lot of assurance in the angel's words to the women. The rebuke is contained in the words "as He said." The women deserved the rebuke. They should have recalled Jesus' promise that He would rise and they should have come to the tomb, not in somber gloom, but with eager expectation. But to their shame, they weren't expecting the resurrection.

The assurance lay in this flat assertion: "He is not here." And it lay in this invitation: "Come, see the place where the Lord lay." There can be a world of significance in a simple verb tense. The angel didn't ask them to see where the Lord was "lying," but where the Lord "lay." "Lying" would have meant He was still there. "Lay" meant He was no longer there.

The angel's message to the women sent them away from that empty tomb "with fear and great joy" (v. 8). They were filled with awe and overwhelmed with joy. The fact that we are two thousand years removed from the event doesn't make it any less marvelous. Shouldn't we also be filled with awe and joy?

The words of many are reported in the Bible. Some of those words are equal in greatness to the words spoken by this angel on the day of Jesus' resurrection. But none is greater. Sin, death, and hell hadn't won. Jesus was victorious over all, and all who know Him through faith share in that victory.

"This Same Jesus. . . Will So Come" (Two Angels)

From God's Word, the Bible...

And while they looked steadfastly toward heaven as He went up, behold, two men stood by them in white apparel, who also said, "Men of Galilee, why do you stand gazing up into heaven? This same Jesus, who was taken up from you into heaven, will so come in like manner as you saw Him go into heaven."

Acts 1:10-11

Days of gladness, days of sadness! Those were the days between Jesus' resurrection and His ascension. The gladness came from the fact that Jesus had gloriously triumphed over the grave. His disciples, slow to believe His promise that He would rise again, were surprised and overjoyed when He did.

But the gladness of those post-resurrection days had to be mingled with sadness as the disciples realized that Jesus would soon leave them once again. The dreaded day arrived—all too quickly in their estimation—and Jesus, after speaking words of assurance to them (vv. 4-5,7-8), was suddenly "taken up" and a cloud received Him out of their sight" (v. 9).

The dreaded moment had come. Jesus was gone, and His disciples must have felt a desperate yearning for Him as they stood staring at that spot where they had last seen Him.

Comfort is what those disciples needed at that moment, and comfort is what they received. The comfort came in the form of two men who weren't really men. Their "white apparel" (v. 10) should make us think of John 20:12, which speaks of "two angels in white" who were sitting in the tomb where Jesus' body had lain.

Angels had come to the sad disciples to give them the assurance that the Jesus who had been taken from them would come again.

There was certainly much in what the angels said to thrill those disciples, and there is much to thrill us if we are Jesus' disciples.

The first thrill is in the "will." The word "will" leaves no room for uncertainty, and that is the word the angels used in regard to Jesus coming again. It will happen.

Many centuries have come and gone since the angels used their "will," and many are the scoffers who cry: "Where is the promise of His coming?" (2 Peter 3:4). These scoffers suggest that the length of time between the promise and its fulfillment negates the promise. To them, the fact that the fulfillment has been so long in coming means it won't come.

The Apostle Peter, who heard the angels deliver their message on that long-ago day, informs us that God doesn't reckon time as we do. What seems to be a very long period of time to us is short to Him (2 Peter 3:8). And Peter assures us that the Lord "is not slack concerning His promise." His delay in fulfilling it doesn't mean it won't be fulfilled. God delays it so He can bring more sinners to repentance (2 Peter 3:9).

Let's not allow ourselves to be influenced by the skeptics but continue to believe with firm faith that the angels' "will" will be fulfilled.

The second thrill in the angels' words to the disciples is in the word "same." The same Jesus who was taken from them that day is the very One who would come for them. It would be the very Jesus whom they had known and loved during His earthly ministry. It would be the Jesus who had been nailed to the cross. It would be the Jesus who was raised from the dead. The Jesus who had come to this earth in our humanity and who had died and risen again in that humanity will come in that same humanity. We will be able to recognize Him by the nail prints in His hands and feet.

The fact that Jesus has gone into heaven in our humanity and will come again in that same humanity means that all of His people will eventually follow Him into heaven in their humanity. Heaven won't be a place where people float around like so many wisps of smoke. It will be God's people dwelling on a new earth in resurrected, glorified bodies.

All of the men and women who saw Jesus ascend to heaven eventually died. Does that mean the angels' promise about Jesus coming again failed for those who died? To the contrary, they will have an advantage when Jesus comes because "the dead in Christ will rise first" (1 Thess. 4:16).

Jesus' coming again will mean resurrection for dead believers and immediate translation from earth to heaven for living believers (1 Thess. 4:17).

What glory awaits those who belong to Christ! We should look forward to it with eager expectation, knowing that we have in the promise of those two angels a true apple of gold in a setting of silver.

October 25

Paul Speaks to a Jailer

From God's Word, the Bible...

So they said, "Believe on the Lord Jesus Christ, and you will be saved, you and your household."

Acts 16:31

Paul and Silas were in prison. The reason? Paul had in the name of Jesus cast a demon out of a young girl (vv. 16-18). Her masters were enraged. They had been using her fortune telling as a way to make a lot of money (vv. 16,19). So these masters complained to the magistrates about Paul and Silas: "These men, being Jews, exceedingly trouble our city" (v. 20).

We should also note that the masters of the young girl had been able to whip a "multitude" into frenzied opposition toward Paul and Silas (v. 22). The magistrates caved in. Setting aside legal proceedings, they ordered Paul and Silas to be beaten and imprisoned (v. 23).

In pain from "many stripes," in prison, and in stocks in the prison! (vv. 23-24)—what a horrible situation for Paul and Silas!

There are several amazing things in this account. It's amazing that Paul could cast out a demon in the name of Jesus. It's amazing that Paul's act could incite so much hatred. It's amazing that the authorities scorned due process and subjected Paul and Silas to such inhumane treatment. But the most amazing thing in my book is this: "But at midnight Paul and Silas were praying and singing hymns to God, and the prisoners were listening to them" (v. 25).

Gordon Keddie says of them: "They had been beaten up, but they were not beaten down!"[3]

The singing and praying of Paul and Silas abruptly ended when "a great earthquake" occurred, throwing all the doors open and snapping all the prisoners' chains (v. 26).

With his prison in shambles and his prisoners gone, the jailer went from earthquake to heart quake. He had been sternly commanded to keep Paul and Silas "securely" (v. 23). He knew his life would count for theirs, so in a flash of despair, he decided to end his life then and there. But wait! The prisoners weren't gone! How he must have rejoiced to hear Paul's loud cry: "Do yourself no harm, for we are all here" (v. 28).

3 Gordon J. Keddie, *You are My Witnesses* (Welwyn Commentary Series), Evangelical Press, 2000, p. 191.

This jailer had almost stepped over the thin line that separates this world from the eternal world. He was suddenly hit with the realization that he had almost stepped into an eternity for which he wasn't prepared. So he "called for a light, ran in, and fell down trembling before Paul and Silas" (v. 29). He then brought them out of the rubble and asked: "Sirs, what must I do to be saved?" (v. 30).

We shouldn't be surprised that he asked this question. God had used the praying and singing of Paul and Silas and the shaking of the earth to make this man realize that they had something he didn't have—and something he urgently needed.

Paul didn't fumble or mumble when the jailer asked his question. He quickly gave the jailer this very plain and simple word: "Believe on the Lord Jesus Christ, and you will be saved, you and your household" (v. 31).

Paul and Silas soon amplified that abbreviated statement as "they spoke the word of the Lord to him and to all who were in his house" (v. 32).

There are three indications that the jailer immediately complied with Paul's words and believed in the Lord Jesus Christ. He took Paul and Silas into his home where he treated their wounds and provided food for them. He and his household were baptized. And he rejoiced in the salvation that he had received (v. 34).

This account speaks with power to believers in Christ. It tells us that we must make it our business to be happy Christians so the Lord can use us as He did Paul and Silas. Every difficulty that comes our way gives us the opportunity to show unbelievers the difference our Christianity makes. This story also shows us that we should always be ready to tell those around us what is necessary for them to be saved.

This story also speaks with power to unbelievers, affirming that the only way to be saved is to believe in the Lord Jesus. No matter how great a sinner one has been, there is salvation for him or her in Christ.

I wouldn't have enjoyed being with Paul and Silas in that prison. But I certainly would have enjoyed hearing Paul say: "Believe on the Lord Jesus Christ, and you will be saved. . . ."

October 26

The Next-to-Last Words of Jesus

From God's Word, the Bible...

"I, Jesus, have sent My angel to testify to you these things in the churches. I am the Root and the Offspring of David, the Bright and Morning Star."

Revelation 22:16

The last recorded words of Jesus in the Bible are found in verse 20 of Revelation 22. We shall come to those. In this reading, we are giving our attention to the next-to-last words of Jesus. They are recorded for us in Revelation 22:16. We might describe this verse as a ton of truth in a small package.

The Lord Jesus is speaking about Himself in this verse. What He has to say should delight each and every child of God. We should note that He begins by calling Himself "Jesus." Here He is appearing to John in all of His glory, and He isn't ashamed of the name that He bore during His time on this earth. That name was associated with all the suffering that He had to endure. It is especially connected with His suffering on the cross. When He was crucified, the placard above His head had these words: "Jesus of Nazareth, the King of the Jews" (John 19:19).

The conclusion we draw is most precious indeed, and that is that Jesus, now in glory, isn't ashamed to be known as Jesus. He is unashamed of His human name because He has carried our humanity into heaven. How often we miss this! Jesus has carried our humanity into heaven! He isn't there now in exactly the same way that He was before He came to this earth. When He took our humanity, He took it forever. And His presence in heaven in our humanity is the guarantee that all who believe in Him will finally follow Him into heaven in resurrected, glorified humanity.

The next thing we should notice is the phrase "My angel." The truth is that the Lord has many angels. The fact that these splendid beings readily and eagerly do His will conveys to us how great our Lord is. He is even now our reigning Lord. The fact that He often doesn't appear to be reigning doesn't mean that He isn't. We will understand it better by and by.

There's yet another phrase that calls for our attention: "to testify to you these things in the churches." While John penned the book of Revelation, he wasn't really the author of it. It was the revelation of the Lord Jesus through John to the churches. It was the Lord testifying to the seven churches that originally received it and to all churches since.

The thing for us to carry away from this is the concern and care that the

Lord Jesus has for His churches. When He left this world, He ascended to join His Father in the glories of heaven. But that doesn't mean He washed His hands of what is going on with His people in this world. Nothing that goes on in His churches is unimportant to Him.

This verse comes to a close with Jesus asserting that He is "the Root and Offspring of David, the Bright and Morning Star."

The first of these two titles, "the Root and Offspring of David," affirms that Jesus is both God and man. The "Root" part of that title means that the Lord Jesus was both the Creator and the Savior of David. In other words, the Lord was the source of both the physical and the spiritual life of David. The "Offspring" part of that title means Jesus, in fulfillment of prophecy, descended from David. To be David's "Root," Jesus had to be God. To be his "Offspring," Jesus had to be a man.

"The Bright and Morning Star" is a marvelous title. Does that mean that Jesus gives light? Yes. But all stars do that. This is a special kind of star. It announces and introduces the coming of day. The Lord Jesus Christ will bring all of His people into never-ending day in heaven. Don Fortner splendidly writes:

> *In that great day, our great Saviour will bring all things to light, and we shall see all things clearly. Then, but not until then, shall we understand all the purposes of God, all the dispensations of providence, all the work of redemption, all the fullness of the covenant, all the glory of grace—and why he saved us.*[4]

It has often been said that last words are very special, and they are. But in the case of the Lord Jesus, I must say that next-to-last words are very special also.

4 Don Fortner, *Discovering Christ in Revelation*, Evangelical Press, 2002, p. 486.

October 27

A Word from the Holy Spirit

From God's Word, the Bible...

And the Spirit and the bride say, "Come!" And let him who hears say, "Come!" And let him who thirsts come. Whoever desires, let him take the water of life freely.

Revelation 22:17

Given the fact that the whole Bible was inspired by the Holy Spirit, we could say the Holy Spirit has spoken a lot. But the Holy Spirit rarely quotes Himself in Scripture. We do have in the verse before us one quote from the Holy Spirit. A simple quote it is, consisting of only one word—"Come!" Since the Lord Jesus spoke in the preceding verse, it only makes sense for the Holy Spirit to urge us to come to Jesus.

It is the unique and special work of the Spirit to exalt the Lord Jesus and to call sinners to Him.

The Spirit's call is warmhearted. "Come" is a warm word. It isn't threatening or frightening.

The Spirit's call is also wide. All are invited to come to Christ. He is the "water of life" (John 4:13-14; 7:37-38) of which we may freely drink, so come and drink freely! The only condition is to be thirsty. Thirsty for forgiveness! Thirsty for right standing with God! Thirsty for eternal life in heaven! If you are thirsty, come and drink! If you are still breathing and still thinking, it isn't too late to come to Christ.

Satan convinces many to refuse the Spirit's invitation because they have been such horrible sinners. Satan tells them that Jesus is only a Savior for those who don't need much saving. He asserts that Jesus is the Savior for only some sinners. In addition to being a colossal lie, that is a despicable insult to Jesus. It suggests that He is a limited and inadequate Savior. Meanwhile, the Bible insists that Jesus can and does save all those who come to Him, no matter how they have plumbed the depths of wickedness. The author of Hebrews writes: ". . . He is also able to save to the uttermost those who come to God through Him, since He ever lives to make intercession for them" (Heb. 7:25).

The word "uttermost" isn't commonly used, but in reference to this matter of salvation, it is one wonderful word. It tells us that the Lord Jesus receives those who are deepest in sin and who are farthest away, and saves them completely and forever.

Jesus Himself expressed the wideness of His salvation when He said: "Come to Me, all you who labor and are heavy laden, and I will give you rest" (Matt. 11:28).

The condition here is that we "labor and are heavy laden." If we're burdened with the weight and the guilt of our sins, we can come to the Lord Jesus with the confidence that He will give us rest. It is not required that we be good sinners or little sinners to be saved—only that we be sinners. These words from Julia H. Johnston express this truth very well.

Marvelous grace of our loving Lord,
Grace that exceeds our sin and our guilt!
Yonder on Calvary's mount outpoured,
There where the blood of the Lamb was spilled.
Grace, grace, God's grace,
Grace that will pardon and cleanse within;
Grace, grace, God's grace,
Grace that is greater than all our sin!
Marvelous, infinite, matchless grace,
Freely bestowed on all who believe!
You that are longing to see His face,
Will you this moment His grace receive?

The only limit imposed on the Lord's ability to save is the one that we ourselves impose by refusing to come to Him.

In addition to the wideness of the invitation, this verse mentions a wideness in the proclamation of the Lord's saving grace. The Spirit urges sinners to come to Christ, and He is joined in that urging by the bride of Christ, that is, by the church. The work of the church is to proclaim the gospel far and wide and to urge sinners to accept it. Many churches and pastors need to be reminded of this.

There's yet more. The individual who has heeded the invitation of the Spirit and the church to come to Christ is invited again—this time to join the Spirit and the church and say to those who are still outside of Christ: "Come!"

To come to Christ means we repent of our sins and trust completely in what He has done for sinners. With the single word "Come," the Holy Spirit calls us to repentance and faith. He calls us to Christ and salvation. He calls us to heaven. What a lovely, delightful word the Holy Spirit has given us! It is an apple of gold.

October 28

The Last Words of Jesus

From God's Word, the Bible...

He who testifies to these things says,
"Surely I am coming quickly."
Amen. Even so, come, Lord Jesus!

Revelation 22:20

This is a special verse. It relates the last words spoken by Jesus in the Bible: "Surely, I am coming quickly." This is the third and final time that Jesus spoke these words. The first time is in verse 7, and the second is in verse 12. The threefold repetition was Jesus' way of emphasizing truth that His people urgently needed.

We must always keep in mind that the book of Revelation was addressed to seven churches in Asia Minor (1:11). These churches were facing trying circumstances and serious challenges. The whole book was designed to give them comfort and encouragement, but they must have found Jesus' assurance that He was coming quickly to be particularly so.

It may seem at first glance that Jesus' words weren't true. Two thousand years have come and gone since Jesus spoke those words. That certainly doesn't seem to equal a quick coming.

One way to deal with this dilemma is to say that Jesus isn't dealing with how soon He will come, but rather the way that He will come when He comes. In other words, when the time finally arrives for Him to come, it will happen very quickly. He will appear without delay and will come in such a way that people will be taken by surprise. And the change that His people will experience will occur "in the twinkling of an eye" (1 Cor. 15:52).

But look again at Jesus' words, and note the present tense. He doesn't say: "I will come." That would certainly be a true statement, but that's not what He says. He says: "Surely, I am coming quickly."

The second coming of Jesus isn't just an event that has to occur. It is a process that has to unfold. That process is laid out for us in Revelation in the form of seven seals, seven trumpets, and seven bowls. Each of these seals, trumpets, and bowls represents God working in history to move us ever closer to the coming of His Son.

The actual event in which Jesus comes has not occurred quickly, but the process that leads to His coming has been unfolding in rapid fashion since the hour that Jesus ascended to the Father in heaven. History hasn't been standing still; it has been steadily marching toward its end.

It's very easy for us to concern ourselves with the wrong thing in regard to the Lord's coming. We tend to get engrossed with the timing of it. We read the word "quickly," and we immediately get caught up in the debate as to whether that is true or false. Jesus quite clearly put the emphasis on a totally different matter—our obedience to His commandments. In verse 7, He says: "Blessed is he who keeps the words of the prophecy of this book." In verse 12, He says: "My reward is with Me, to give to every one according to his work."

When the Bible deals with the Lord's return, it doesn't lay the stress on *when* but rather on *how*. It doesn't encourage us to ask when the Lord's coming will occur. It rather encourages us to ask ourselves how we are living. Are we tampering and trifling with His Word or giving serious and careful attention to it? Are we mindful of the fact that obedience will bring rich rewards from our Lord, and disobedience will cause the loss of those rewards?

To put it another way, the truth of the Lord's coming ought to make us think seriously and carefully about these words from the Apostle Peter: ". . .what manner of persons ought you to be in holy conduct and godliness. . ." (2 Peter 3:11).

The last recorded words of Jesus—how encouraging they are! The Lord Jesus is even now in the process of coming. World events are not meaningless. The Lord is working in and through them to prepare the stage for His appearance. Our response to these things should be to say: "Are You, Lord, in the process of coming? Continue the process until it is finally complete, and we finally see Your dear face in glory." In other words, our response should be to join John in saying: "Amen. Even so, come Lord Jesus!"

October 29

An Apple of Gold from a Rotten Apple (1)

FROM GOD'S WORD, THE BIBLE...

And one of them, Caiaphas, being high priest that year, said to them, "You know nothing at all, nor do you consider that it is expedient for us that one man should die for the people, and not that the whole nation should perish."

JOHN 11:49-50

Sometimes truth comes from unusual places. In the verses above, the Gospel of John gives us a couple of examples of this. Caiaphas and Pilate were anything but good men. They weren't men who had a close and familiar association with the truth. But on the occasions reported in these verses, they spoke marvelous truths about Jesus. It is always an apple of gold when the truth is spoken about Jesus. So, Caiaphas and Pilate give us apples of gold even though they were rotten apples.

We will look at Pilate in our next reading. Let me introduce you now to Caiaphas. Don't shake his hand. If you do, you will have to immediately wash your hand. This Caiaphas was one slimy fellow. It wouldn't seem so. It shouldn't have been so. Caiaphas was holding the highest office that Jewish religion had to offer. He was the high priest. A man holding such a high office should be high in virtue and integrity. Not Caiaphas! This man treasured murder in his heart, and urged others to treasure it as well.

Jesus had just raised Lazarus from the dead even though he had been in the grave for four days. That act put the cat among the pigeons. It caused many to believe in Jesus (v. 45). The religious leaders of Israel knew they had to do something about Jesus. If they left Him alone, more and more would follow Him, and when the Romans learned that multitudes of Jews were acknowledging Jesus as their king, well, they wouldn't be happy.

The dilemma of what to do with Jesus prompted Caiaphas to offer his murderous assessment: Jesus must die! Caiaphas was speaking as a political man who was concerned with political realities, but he inadvertently spoke the truth. Here's part of what he said: ". . . it is expedient that one man should die for the people, and not that the whole nation should perish" (v. 50).

To Caiaphas, it was Jesus or the nation. If Jesus didn't die, the nation would, and he, Caiaphas, would much sooner part with Jesus than with the nation.

John, the author of this Gospel, couldn't wait to jump on that. After relating Caiaphas' words, John quickly added these words: "Now this he did not say on his own authority; but being high priest that year he prophesied that

Jesus would die for the nation, and not for that nation only, but also that He would gather together in one the children of God who were scattered abroad" (vv. 51-52).

In trying to rid himself of Jesus, Caiaphas had preached the gospel! Had he realized it, he would have been mortified. Had he realized his blunder, he might have felt like removing his unruly tongue so he could never repeat the blunder again.

There have been many wonderful preachers of the gospel through the centuries. The names of George Whitefield, Charles Spurgeon, Jonathan Edwards, and Martyn Lloyd-Jones easily come to mind. Should we add Caiaphas to that list? Imagine it! Caiaphas, a preacher of the gospel! Who could have guessed it?

But, of course, Caiaphas didn't preach the gospel knowingly and willingly. He blundered into the truth of the gospel. He didn't speak "on his own authority." It was God who was speaking through the evil Caiaphas at this moment.

What is the gospel? It is the good news of Jesus dying for others so they don't have to die. It is Jesus dying as a substitute for others. It is as Caiaphas said!

We aren't talking here about Jesus dying physically so others wouldn't have to die physically. It is much more profound than that. We're talking about Jesus dying a special kind of death—one in which He received the wrath of God that sinners themselves will receive in eternity if they don't receive Him.

We don't know what became of Caiaphas. We can hope that, after Jesus died, he recalled his own words and understood them, not in the political way that he originally had in mind, but rather on the higher level of Jesus dying as the substitute for sinners. We can hope that Caiaphas came to believe that Jesus died for him and that he laid hold of that with real faith. We can hope that Caiaphas will be in heaven. While we wait to see if he is, let's rejoice in the apple of gold that he left us in a setting of silver—his statement of the gospel.

October 30

An Apple of Gold from a Rotten Apple (2)

From God's Word, the Bible…

Pilate said to Him, "What is truth?" And when he had said this, he went out again to the Jews, and said to them, "I find no fault in Him at all."

John 18:38

Pontius Pilate was the big Roman in the land of Israel. He governed the Jews as the representative of the Roman Empire. When we meet him in John's Gospel, he has a very complex problem on his hands—Jesus!

The religious leaders of the Jews had taken Jesus into custody, had "tried" Him and found Him worthy of death. But the Jews weren't to execute criminals without approval from Rome. So, they brought Jesus to Pilate along with a charge that they knew would resonate with Pilate, namely, that Jesus was claiming to be a king (Luke 23:2). A Roman governor would have to take that seriously because Caesar didn't like having rival kings around. So Pilate began his interrogation of Jesus by asking Him: "Are you the King of the Jews?" (v. 33).

After interrogating Jesus three times, Pilate said to the Jewish leaders: "I find no fault in Him." Pilate certainly didn't intend those words to be a theological statement about Jesus. He was merely concerned with legalities and politics. He was merely offering his assessment that there was no legal basis for even holding Jesus, much less for executing Him.

As far as theological truth was concerned, Pilate couldn't have cared less. A few minutes before announcing his finding to the Jews, Pilate had walked away from Jesus with a casual shrug and the question: "What is truth?" (v. 38).

But while Pilate didn't intend to make a theological statement about Jesus, that's exactly what he did. There is no fault to be found in Jesus. There was no legal fault to be found in Jesus. He hadn't broken any of Rome's laws. But we must go further. There is no moral fault in Jesus. He was completely without sin. Jesus is the only person who has lived perfectly. He never thought an evil thought, never spoke a wrong word, and never did a sinful thing. He is, in the words of the Apostle Peter, "a lamb without blemish and without spot" (1 Peter 1:19).

There was a time in which most professing Christians considered the sinless life of Jesus to be an indispensable link in the chain of redemption. Several years ago, most Christians would have readily agreed that if the link of Jesus' sinlessness is broken, the whole of redemption is irretrievably broken.

But things have changed. Surveys in recent years have revealed serious slippage at this point with many who profess faith in Christ now saying He probably committed sins, or, to put it in a more sanitary fashion, "made mistakes."

Count me among those who are unwilling to give up the sinlessness of Christ, and among those who believe that it is still an essential link in the chain of redemption. To me, it is quite simple. Jesus came to this earth to pay the penalty for sinners. If He had been guilty of sin Himself, He would have had to pay the penalty for Himself and, therefore, could not have paid the penalty for others.

We must always keep this in mind: part of what Jesus came to this earth to do was to provide the very righteousness that God demands of sinners. God requires it, but we don't' have it. Jesus, on the other hand, did have it, and God in grace counts the righteousness of Christ as though it were ours when we come to Christ in repentance and faith.

Jesus gave testimony to His own sinlessness when He boldly asked the religious leaders this question: "Which of you convicts Me of sin?" (John 8:46a). Jesus could never have asked that question if He had the slightest bit of uncertainty about His performance. The fact that He did ask it tells us that He knew there was no sin to be found in Him. A bit earlier, He had said to those same men: "I always do those things that please Him" (v. 29). And the "Him" to whom He was referring was His Father.

This wasn't brazen arrogance on the part of Jesus. It was merely a statement of fact. We should accept it as a fact and rejoice in it.

Are we grateful that Pilate had no interest in discovering the truth about Jesus? No, but we should be grateful that, in the midst of His political maneuverings, He stated for us the truth about Jesus. There was no fault in Jesus, but there is fault in us; that's why we need a sinless, perfect Savior such as Jesus. Is He your Lord and Savior? Have you turned from sin and are you trusting in Him alone?

October 31

A Truly Rotten Apple from A Truly Rotten Apple

FROM GOD'S WORD, THE BIBLE...

Now the serpent was more cunning than any beast of the field which the Lord God had made. And he said to the woman, "Has God indeed said, 'You shall not eat of every tree of the garden'?"
Then the serpent said to the woman, "You will not surely die. For God knows that in the day you eat of it your eyes will be opened, and you will be like God, knowing good and evil."

GENESIS 3:1, 4-5

It has been our blessing and privilege to notice several fitly spoken words in the Bible. The Book of Proverbs calls these "apples of gold." Jesus spoke most of the words we have noticed. That shouldn't surprise us. Jesus, the greatest person who ever lived, spoke the greatest words ever spoken. But we have also found opportunities to notice words from the Father, the Holy Spirit, angels, and men. We have even come across a couple of apples of gold from very evil men.

We now come to the end of this volume by listening to someone we have not yet heard from—Satan. In the opening verses of Genesis 3, we come upon Satan speaking. His words are as distorted as he is. They can never be called "apples of gold." It is far more fitting to refer to his words as rotten words. Since he is such a thoroughly rotten being, we have in his words a truly rotten apple from a truly rotten apple. His words were rotten because they came from his rotten mouth.

Satan is still speaking rotten words. He does so when he prompts people to indulge in blasphemy, profanity, gossip, and complaining. He is very active in prompting ministers to distort and deny the gospel of Christ. But Satan has never spoken more rotten, evil words than he did in the garden of Eden. Those words were spoken to an audience of one, but they have affected every human being since.

Satan came to Eve in the form of a serpent, which may have originally been the most beautiful of all the animals God made. By coming in this attractive form, Satan was probably hoping to catch Eve off guard.

The first rotten words Satan spoke questioned the goodness of God: "Has God indeed said, 'You shall not eat of every tree of the garden'?" (v. 1). Satan was insinuating that God wasn't as good as Adam and Eve thought Him to be. He was holding something back from them! A truly good God would deny them nothing! He would have given them access to every single tree of the garden without so much as a single exception.

Satan still enjoys attacking the goodness of God. When a difficulty comes our way, he is quick to say: "Ah, you see, you are facing this thing because God doesn't really care for you."

Sadly enough, multitudes of people believe his lie.

The next rotten words that came from Satan's mouth flatly denied the truth of God's Word. When Satan asked if Eve was free to eat of all the trees of the garden, she replied: "We may eat the fruit of the trees of the garden; but of the fruit of the tree which is in the midst of the garden, God has said, 'You shall not eat it, nor shall you touch it, lest you die'" (vv. 2-3).

That was fairly close to being accurate. God had definitely told Adam and Eve to not eat of the tree, but, so far as we know, He hadn't told them to not touch it (2:17).

Satan's response was swift and brazen: "You will not surely die" (v. 4).

God had spoken, and Satan contradicted Him. Satan is still doing this. Every denial of the truth of God's Word has his leering face behind it.

Yes, God had forbidden Adam and Eve to eat of the tree of knowledge of good and evil, but it wasn't to be unkind to them. He made them with free will. For the will to be truly free, it has to have a choice to make. God could have made Adam and Eve mere machines that had no choice but to love and obey Him. But He made them so they would have to choose to obey Him. The fact that God made them this way was an expression of His goodness to them—just the opposite of what Satan said.

And, yes, the penalty for their disobedience was death in all of its forms—physical, spiritual, and eternal. Spiritual death was the central thing. It is alienation from God and it results in physical and eternal death.

Satan's words to Eve were the rottenest ever spoken because they brought death upon Adam and Eve and all their descendants. But good came from those rotten words. In response to them, God answered with this apple of gold—"Christ!"

As we draw this book to a conclusion, let us think of One who was to come as the Second Adam and who would be the Savior of sinners—the Lord Jesus Christ. Satan tried to tempt Him, too, but without any success. God was true to His promise that Jesus would crush the head of Satan. He did that at Calvary when He bore the sins of all who would ever turn away from sin and trust Him as Lord and Savior. And He still saves sinners today. Has He saved you? He is a willing and able Savior. Come to Him in repentance and faith right now!

THE MONTH OF NOVEMBER

Old Houses, New Houses

... And 30 Other Bible-Based Meditations

It was finally gone, the victim of the cold steel of a bulldozer's blade. I knew the end was rapidly approaching, but I still hated to see it go. I'm talking about the little old house in which I spent the first twenty-one years of my life. Little? Yes. It consisted of a kitchen, a living room, two bedrooms, a pantry and a porch. Oh, yes, there was also that little area on one side that my mother referred to as "the sun room."

Contents

Old Houses, New Houses

From God's Word, the Bible...

"In My Father's house are many mansions; if it were not so, I would have told you. I go to prepare a place for you."

For we know that if our earthly house, this tent, is destroyed, we have a building from God, a house not made with hands, eternal in the heavens.

John 14:2; 2 Corinthians 5:1

It was finally gone, the victim of the cold steel of a bulldozer's blade. I knew the end was rapidly approaching, but I still hated to see it go.

I'm talking about the little old house in which I spent the first twenty-one years of my life. Little? Yes. It consisted of a kitchen, a living room, two bedrooms, a pantry, and a porch. Oh, yes, there was also that little area on one side that my mother referred to as "the sun room."

What about the bathroom? There was no bathroom. We used the privy, which was situated a little way down the hill. My folks, you see, were very poor. We just had enough money, as they put it, "to make ends meet."

The old house was in bad condition all through my young years. Walking across the floor would cause it to sort of creak and groan as if it were offering a protest against the person who was adding more weight to its weary existence. The walls were adorned with various cracks and holes. And the foundation could only see its sturdy days in the rear-view mirror.

But I loved that old house. It wasn't the physical structure that made it lovable. It was rather what went on there. The love and respect we had for each other, the happiness and the laughter, the gratitude we felt for the Lord's blessings, and our shared faith in the precious gospel of Christ—all of these things and many more made the old house a palace of delight.

One of the most pleasant memories of my childhood is my mother filling that old house with singing before Parkinson's disease made her body like the house itself—weak, weary, and worn.

I treasure the lessons that I learned in my years in the old house, one of which was that it isn't necessary to have lots of money to be rich. Greater still was this lesson: believers in Christ have two new houses awaiting them. One is a new body. Paul says we have "a building from God, a house not made with hands, eternal in the heavens" (2 Cor. 5:1). My body is an "earthly house," a "tent," which will be "destroyed." But when Jesus comes I will receive a new body (Phil. 3:20-21).

The second house believers will receive is the "Father's house" (John 14:1). That term is Jesus' shorthand for our eternal home that is so beautifully described for us in Revelation 21 and 22.

Here, then, is the final outcome for believers in Christ—we will live in new bodies on a new earth. Those bodies will be beyond the reach of disease and death. No Parkinson's in heaven, and no death either! Thank God! And the new earth will be beyond the reach of sin and Satan. The Apostle Peter refers to it as "an inheritance" that is "incorruptible and undefiled." He also says that it "does not fade away," but it is "reserved in heaven" for us (1 Peter 1:4).

Christians have indescribable glory awaiting them, and it's all because of the Lord Jesus Christ. He came from heaven's glory to this earth to take us from this earth to heaven's glory.

When will believers in Christ receive their new houses? When Jesus comes! One glorious day, He will break through the clouds "with a shout, with the voice of an archangel, and with the trumpet of God" (1 Thess. 4:16). Dead believers will hear the voice of their Lord, and they will spring from their graves in marvelous resurrection life. Living believers will be "caught up" (1 Thess. 4:17). They will instantaneously receive their new bodies without having to pass through death. And then the Lord will escort all of His people to their new house in heaven. New bodies on a new earth—what a destiny!

As we wait for the glory of that day, we live in this world of change and decay. Nothing here lasts. How thankful we should be that we have the Lord to abide with us! Before her disease took her voice, my mother used to sing:

Swift to its close ebbs out life's little day;
Earth's joys grow dim, its glories pass away;
Change and decay in all around I see:
O Thou who changest not, abide with me!
(Henry F. Lyte)

November 2

The Faith Chapter

From God's Word, the Bible...

*Now faith is the substance of things hoped for,
the evidence of things not seen.*

Hebrews 11:1

Faith, hope, and love are often linked together in Scripture. It is interesting that one chapter of Scripture is devoted to each of these graces. Romans 8 is the hope chapter; 1 Corinthians 13 is the love chapter; and Hebrews 11 is the faith chapter.

The author writes: "Now faith is the substance of things hoped for, the evidence of things not seen" (v. 1). In other words, faith is the assurance that the things God has promised are true and certain. It treats them as being solid and real even though they are at this time unseen and unfulfilled. John Calvin says faith gives the believer "a sure and secure possession of those things which God has promised."

The New International Version translates verse 1 in this way: "Now faith is being sure of what we hope for and certain of what we do not see."

The author himself further defines faith as he makes reference to the great heroes of the faith: "These all died in faith, not having received the promises, but having seen them afar off were assured of them, embraced them, and confessed that they were strangers and pilgrims on the earth" (v. 12).

Many mistake faith for mere positive thinking. They think faith is selecting something we want to be true and convincing ourselves that it will be true. But that's not faith. Faith is rather believing what God has said. Faith cannot function in a vacuum. It functions on the basis of the Word of God (Rom. 10:17). Faith is sure because God has promised.

When we go through the list of the men and women of faith that the author of Hebrews mentions, we see that each one believed something that God had revealed.

Think about Abel (v. 4). Before he was born, God revealed the kind of sacrifice that was acceptable to Him, namely, a blood sacrifice (Gen. 3:21). Undoubtedly, Abel learned about this revelation from his parents, accepted it and acted on the basis of it.

Then there's Noah (v. 7), who was told by God that the flood was going to come on the earth. He believed this revelation and built the ark.

Abraham (vv. 8-10) was told by God to leave his homeland and go to a new country (Gen. 12:1-4), and he acted on the basis of that word. He also received from God the revelation that the future holds for believers something far better than anything this life has to offer, that is, "the city which has foundations, whose builder and maker is God" (v. 10). Abraham also believed that promise and eagerly looked forward to its fulfillment.

Sarah (vv. 11-12) and Abraham received from God the definite promise that she would conceive and bear a son in her old age, and this son would be the one through whom the promises God made to Abraham would be fulfilled (Gen. 18:9-15). The fact that Sarah laughed when she heard this promise indicates that one can have real faith and still waver. Weak faith is still faith.

The greatest test of Abraham's faith came when God commanded him to sacrifice Isaac (vv. 17-19). Abraham knew that Isaac had to survive because God had clearly said: "In Isaac your seed shall be called" (v. 18; Gen. 21:12), and at this point Isaac himself had no children.

Because Abraham knew Isaac had to survive, he concluded that if he indeed had to sacrifice Isaac, God would have to raise him from the dead (v. 19). God, of course, provided a ram for Abraham to sacrifice instead of Isaac (Gen. 22:13). God's purpose in all this was to point Abraham and Isaac ahead to the redeeming death of the Lord Jesus Christ.

Moses (vv. 23-29), knowing that God had promised to deliver the people of Israel from bondage in Egypt, left his life in Egypt behind and identified himself with the people of God (vv. 24-27). After receiving clear instructions from God, he led the people of Israel in the observance of the Passover (v. 28) and also across the Red Sea (v. 29).

All these heroes of the faith join their voices to urge us to believe the Word of God, no matter how foolish it may seem to do so. And they also remind us that while true faith may struggle and waver, it can never be extinguished.

The Bible emphasizes that faith—saving faith—is always to be put in the Lord Jesus Christ. He is the great Savior of sinners. Each of the people in today's reading looked ahead to the coming of the One whom God had appointed to live and die in their place—and to rise again as the Lord, victorious over death. Is your faith in Him alone?

November 3

The Hope Chapter

From God's Word, the Bible...

For we were saved in this hope, but hope that is seen is not hope; for why does one still hope for what he sees? But if we hope for what we do not see, we eagerly wait for it with perseverance.

Romans 8:24-25

Romans 8 is the hope chapter of the Bible. While the word "hope" itself is mentioned only six times in its thirty-nine verses, the theme of hope permeates almost the entire chapter.

Paul asserts that Christians are saved in hope (v. 24). When Christians are saved, they are placed in the realm of hope. They live out the remainder of their lives in that realm.

That won't seem to be such a great thing if we fail to understand the meaning of hope. To us, hope conveys possible doubt or uncertainty. Someone says he is hoping to get a good report from the doctor. The person who says that isn't sure; the report may be good or bad.

We sometimes hear people say this: "All we can do is hope for the best." That phrase is often used in serious situations in which the outcome is in doubt. We also hear people say: "Hope for the best and expect the worst." That means the outcome of a particular situation is up in the air.

Our modern use of the word "hope" is not the same as that of the Bible. To us, hope is weak. In the Bible, it is strong. We will understand hope better if we place it alongside faith. Faith is the calm assurance that all the things that God has promised will prove to be true. It views them as being solid and real even though they are now unseen and unfulfilled. Faith is certainty.

In the Bible, hope goes beyond faith. Faith says: "I am sure this will happen." Hope says: "I can't wait to see it." Hope is eager expectation. It is the believer standing on tiptoe and craning his neck to see that thing which faith makes him or her certain of.

In Romans 8, the Apostle Paul mentions two things that the Christian is ever so eager to see. One is the redemption of all creation (vv. 18-22); the other is the redemption of the body (vv. 23-25).

In my years as a pastor, I was often surprised to discover that many churchgoers seem to have little or no understanding of the redemption of creation.

The natural realm is not as God made it. All of creation fell when Adam fell. Paul refers to it as being "subjected to futility, not willingly" (v. 20).

Through no fault of its own, creation was seriously damaged by human sin. Paul also refers to it as being in "bondage" (v. 21).

That is not the final word for this natural order. Paul tells us that this earth is eagerly awaiting "the glorious liberty of the children of God" (v. 21) because it will share in that liberty. Creation itself will finally be delivered from its fallen condition. When the end comes, it will be restored to its original beauty and glory. God's work of salvation consists of Him restoring what Satan has ruined. That includes this earth. If God doesn't put the earth back to where it was before sin entered, Satan will have won a tremendous victory.

The other thing that the Christian is eager to see is the redemption of the body.

Just as creation was affected by sin, so was the human body. It is so feeble and frail and prone to disease. All of this is the result of sin. So as creation groans in anticipation of its redemption, so we groan within ourselves as we wait for the redemption of our bodies.

When a Christian dies, the soul immediately goes to be with the Lord and the body goes into the grave. There the body will remain until Jesus comes. When He comes, He will bring with Him the souls of all dead believers, will raise their bodies from their graves, and reunite souls and bodies. On that day, Jesus won't merely resuscitate our bodies so we can resume life as we knew it before. It will be so we can begin a whole new kind of existence. We will have bodies like the resurrection body of Jesus, and in those bodies we will live on the earth that has itself been redeemed (Phil. 3:20-21; 1 Thess. 4:13-18; 1 John 3:1-2).

A new body on a new earth! This is the glorious future of the Christian!

And it is all because of the redeeming work of Christ. Each believer should look back on His life and death with great gratitude and look forward to the future, saying: "Bring it on! I can't wait to see it!"

November 4

The Love Chapter

From God's Word, the Bible...

Though I speak with the tongues of men and of angels, but have not love, I have become sounding brass or a clanging cymbal.

1 Corinthians 13:1

There's no debate that 1 Corinthians 13 is the love chapter of the Bible. In beautiful and moving words, Paul calls the believers in Corinth away from their fascination with spiritual gifts to the higher priority of love. It is, in the words of Paul, "a more excellent way" (12:31).

What is love? It is having such a strong affection for others that we give ourselves to doing that which is in their best interest.

In verses 4-7, Paul lays out fifteen characteristics of love. When we see someone demonstrating these characteristics we are seeing that person practicing or manifesting love. Paul tells us that love:

- suffers long—it's slow to anger as it puts up with that which is unpleasant and distasteful in other people;
- is kind—it is gracious and tender, like the Lord Jesus;
- doesn't envy—it isn't unhappy when others succeed;
- doesn't parade itself—it doesn't allow us to live for notice and applause;
- isn't puffed up—it doesn't allow us to be so full of ourselves that we act arrogantly and talk conceitedly;
- doesn't behave rudely—it's so gentle and sensitive that it refuses to do things that bring shame or embarrassment to others;
- doesn't seek its own—it doesn't insist on its own way but constantly insists on seeking the wellbeing of others;
- isn't provoked—it's not irritable, temperamental, touchy, thin-skinned, or easily offended;
- thinks no evil—it doesn't keep a record of wrongs;
- doesn't rejoice in iniquity—it doesn't receive pleasure from the failures and misfortunes of others;
- rejoices in the truth—it is always happy to see the truth win;
- bears all things—it passes over in silence and keeps confidential that which is repugnant in others;
- believes all things—it's always ready to see the best in others and to give them the benefit of the doubt;
- hopes all things—it isn't pessimistic about those who have been troublesome in the past, that is, it doesn't easily give up on others;

- endures all things—it refuses to be dismayed and conquered.

Why did Paul go into such detail to describe love? He wanted his readers to see that *love outperforms all the spiritual gifts*. It's possible to have spiritual gifts without demonstrating these wonderful qualities, but it's not possible to have love without demonstrating them.

Paul closes the chapter with another emphasis—*love outlasts the gifts* (vv. 8-13). The Apostle points his readers to the coming of "that which is perfect" (v. 10), that is, to the coming of the perfect eternal day when believers in Christ will see God face to face and all things will be made clear (v. 12). On that day, all partial things will be put away (v. 10) because that which is partial is not perfect.

The putting away of partial things will mean the putting away of the gifts. Prophecy, tongues, and knowledge (the ability to grasp and communicate God's Word in a special way) will have no place in heaven. But when the gifts are gone, the graces will abide. We will exercise faith in heaven as we continue to depend on God to provide for us. We will exercise hope in heaven as we eagerly look forward to discovering more of its treasures. But while faith and hope will be in heaven, they will not surpass love.

Why will love be greater in heaven than faith and hope? It makes us like God. God doesn't have faith or hope, but He is love.

In Paul's list of love's qualities, we see the Lord Jesus, who is the only person who has ever perfectly practiced them. We should know that we will never be able to perfectly practice true love in this life as He did. We should also know that we should be ever striving to follow His example. We don't really have Him as our example if we haven't taken Him as our Lord and Savior.

To love as God loves, we must know God through repenting of our sins and trusting in His Son. The Apostle John says: "Beloved, let us love one another, for love is of God, and everyone who loves is born of God and knows God. . . . In this is love, not that we loved God, but that He loved us and sent His Son to be the propitiation for our sins" (1 John 4:7,10).

November 5

Three Cheers from Jesus

FROM GOD'S WORD, THE BIBLE...

So He got into a boat, crossed over, and came to His own city. Then behold, they brought to Him a paralytic lying on a bed. When Jesus saw their faith, He said to the paralytic, "Son, be of good cheer; your sins are forgiven you."

But Jesus turned around, and when He saw her He said, "Be of good cheer, daughter; your faith has made you well." And the woman was made well from that hour.

But immediately Jesus spoke to them, saying, "Be of good cheer! It is I; do not be afraid."

MATTHEW 9:1-2,22; 14:27

The Gospel of Matthew reports three occasions on which Jesus said: "Be of good cheer." On each of those occasions, Jesus was speaking to an individual or a group who were beaten down and on the verge of despair.

On the first occasion, Jesus spoke to a man who had been paralyzed for a long time. On the second occasion, He spoke to a woman who for twelve years had suffered from a hemorrhage. On the third occasion, He spoke to His disciples who were trying to pilot their little boat through a stormy sea.

What are the truths that we can draw from these situations? The first is this: *We can be of good cheer because Jesus forgives sin* (9:1-2).

In this passage we have a paralyzed man lying on his bed, and Jesus says: "Be of good cheer; your sins are forgiven you."

What does this say to us? The answer couldn't be plainer. It affirms that Jesus regarded this man's spiritual condition as being more important than his physical condition. That's not to say that Jesus wasn't interested in his physical condition. He was, and He proved it by healing him. But that's not where Jesus started. No one had said a word to Jesus about forgiving this man's sins, but that is where Jesus began.

Jesus put the emphasis in the right place. We all have to leave this world and meet God. No one will be able to stand in God's holy presence unless his sins are forgiven. The good news that emerges from Jesus' dealings with the paralyzed man is this: Jesus can and does forgive sins. He came to this earth for the express purpose of providing the way for our sins to be forgiven. He did so by dying on the cross. There He received the penalty for sinners so that all who come to Him in repentance and faith will never receive that same penalty but will rather receive forgiveness.

The second truth we see from the three cheers of Jesus is this: *We can be of good cheer because Jesus values imperfect faith* (9:22).

The woman who had suffered for twelve years with "a flow of blood" (9:20) quite obviously had imperfect faith. Her faith that Jesus could heal her was mixed up with some superstition. She seems to have regarded Jesus as something of a magician who exuded power to those who touched Him. So, she managed to work her way through the crowd around Jesus and touch Him. And that touch was rewarded as Jesus healed her.

We can and should be thankful that the Lord doesn't require us to have perfect faith before He saves us. Weak faith is still faith. What a consolation that is! J.C. Ryle writes:

> Our faith may be feeble; our courage may be small; our grasp of the Gospel and its promises, may be weak and trembling,—but, after all, the grand question is, Do we really trust only in Christ? Do we look to Jesus, and only to Jesus, for pardon and peace? If this be so, it is well.[5]

The truth we discover from Jesus' third cheering statement is very comforting, namely, *We can be of good cheer because Jesus is with us in the storms of life* (14:27).

After feeding a multitude of five thousand, Jesus told His disciples to cross the Sea of Galilee. They soon encountered a ferocious storm. The boat "was now in the middle of the sea, tossed by waves, for the wind was contrary" (14:24).

Jesus came to His disciples by walking on the sea. His first words to them were: "Be of good cheer! It is I; do not be afraid."

Jesus did marvelous things in that storm. He enabled Simon Peter to walk toward Him on the water and then rescued him when, after a good start, he began to sink. Jesus then stepped with Simon into the boat, and the wind immediately ceased (14:28-32).

We have our storms, too. And they can be very threatening and frightening. But the Lord Jesus has promised to be with us all through this life (Heb. 13:5), and that includes the storms. With Him beside us, our fear can give away to cheer.

These three passages put the Lord Jesus on display. We see His perfect knowledge, His abounding sympathy, and His sovereign authority and power. Our response should be to worship Him as His disciples did when He stilled the storm (14:33).

5 J.C. Ryle, *Expository Thoughts on Matthew*, The Banner of Truth Trust, Edinburgh, 1995, p. 89.

November 6

From Lucifer to Satan

FROM GOD'S WORD, THE BIBLE...

We know that we are of God, and the whole world lies under the sway of the wicked one. And we know that the Son of God has come and has given us an understanding, that we may know Him who is true; and we are in Him who is true, in His Son Jesus Christ. This is the true God and eternal life.

1 JOHN 5:19-20

The name "Satan" means "adversary." There is a real person that the Bible calls "Satan." He is the adversary of God and of the people of God. He hates each with equal passion. Where did Satan come from? He didn't start out as Satan. Far from it! He started out as Lucifer, which means "morning star" or "day star." He was one of the many angels that God created to serve Him. But it's not enough to say that he was one of the angels. He was supreme among the angels as these words indicate:

You were the seal of perfection,
Full of wisdom and perfect in beauty. . .
You were the anointed cherub who covers. . .
You were perfect in your ways from the day you were created. . . .
(EZEK. 28:12,14,15)

Jonathan Edwards understood the phrase "the anointed cherub that covers" to indicate that Lucifer enjoyed special status in heaven, standing next to the very throne of God. Edwards writes:

> . . .before the fall of this cherub he is spoken of as being alone entitled to this great honour and nearness to God's throne in heaven, that he was anointed to be above his fellows.[6]

But Lucifer didn't retain his exalted name and position. He became Satan. How did he go from morning star to adversary? The Bible answers by telling us Lucifer developed "I" trouble. Notice how he uses the word "I" five times in Isaiah 14:13-14.

6 Jonathan Edwards, *The Works of Jonathan Edwards* (Edinburgh, UK: The Banner of Truth Trust, 1988), vol. ii, p.609.

I will ascend into heaven,
I will exalt my throne above the stars of God;
I will also sit on the mount of the congregation.
I will ascend above the heights of the clouds,
I will be like the Most High.
(Isa. 14:13-14)

The first sin that ever occurred was not when Adam and Eve disobeyed God in the Garden of Eden. It took place in the heart of Lucifer before this world was created. It was pride.

I have to connect the sin of Lucifer with God's plan of redemption. We know that plan was put in place before the world began. God knew that He would create this world as well as Adam and Eve. He also knew that Adam and Eve would fall into sin. So before there was a world and before there was a man, God put in place His marvelous plan of salvation. The three persons of the Trinity developed this plan in which each would play a part. The centerpiece of this plan was the Son coming to this earth in our humanity, living in perfect obedience to God, dying on the cross, and rising again.

That plan was not only formulated in heaven. It was also announced in heaven. The angels were told that the Son would step into this earth as a man and that they would have to worship and serve Him in His humanity as well as minister to human beings.

That was too much for Lucifer. His pride wouldn't allow him to serve the Son in human form and other human beings. That was beneath him! Jonathan Edwards writes of Lucifer:

> But when it was revealed to him, high and glorious as he was, that he must be a ministering spirit to the race of mankind which he had seen newly created, which appeared so feeble, mean, and despicable, so vastly inferior, . . .he could not bear it. This occasioned his fall. . . .[7]

Dissatisfied with God's plan, Lucifer made a plan of his own. He would overthrow God and take His place. Although he was joined in his rebellion by one third of all the angels (Rev. 12:4), the whole enterprise came crashing down. Lucifer and his followers were expelled from heaven (Rev. 12:7-9).

Lucifer's plan failed and God's plan went forward. But Satan is still alive, and he is still opposing God and God's people. Why does God allow him to do so? We don't have all the answers we would like. We have to wait for those. Instead of dwelling on what we don't know, we should dwell on what we do know—God is greater than Satan. He defeated him when he first rebelled. He defeated him again when Jesus died on the cross (Col. 2:15). And He will defeat him yet again at the end of human history (Rev. 20:10).

7 Edwards, vol. ii, p.610.

November 7

The Bible in the Toilet

From God's Word, the Bible...

Forever, O Lord,
Your word is settled in heaven.

Psalm 119:89

I had placed my Bible on a table in the church foyer a few minutes before our evening worship service was to begin. But when I went back, it was gone. I asked a couple of the church members if they knew what happened to my Bible. It was then that I learned that two young men had come into the church. It soon became clear that they weren't there to worship but rather to ridicule and threaten. They were invited to stay for the service, but they refused to do so, and parted with a few comments about how stupid all of us were to believe and practice what they referred to as "this stuff."

They were gone and my Bible was gone. Had they taken it with them? Several people fanned out across the building to look for the missing Bible. One of the men soon returned to say he had found it. It was stuffed in the toilet in the men's room.

Having attended a secular university, I was used to being around Christian-haters, but I was still a little surprised at what these young ruffians had done with my Bible. That was a long time ago. Hatred of Christianity has grown so much the last several years that I wouldn't be surprised at all if the same thing were to happen to me today.

The prophet Jeremiah had an experience similar to mine. We read about it in Jeremiah 36. The Lord commanded Jeremiah to write on a scroll the words that He, the Lord, had given Jeremiah to speak (v. 1).

We have in this command a small picture of how the whole Bible came to exist. God prompted men to write what He wanted written (2 Tim. 3:16; 2 Peter 1:21).

When the scroll was completed, it was read at the temple "in the hearing of all the people" (v. 10). It was then read to the princes of the kingdom. These men were filled with fear as they listened to this reading because Jeremiah's scroll contained the message of God's judgment (vv. 11-19).

These princes decided that the scroll should be read to King Jehoiakim, who was sitting "in the winter house in the ninth month, with a fire burning on the hearth before him" (v. 22).

Jehoiakim's response to this is shocking: he listened to part of the reading and then "cut it with the scribe's knife and cast it into the fire that was on the hearth" (v. 23).

The princes who had wanted the scroll read to the king were astonished at the attitude of the king and his attendants. The king had burned the scroll, which was presented to him as God's Word, but the king and his attendants "were not afraid, nor did they tear their garments" (v. 24).

The king even went so far as to command that Jeremiah and his secretary, Baruch, be arrested (v. 26). Such was his disdain for the Word of God and the men of God!

Jeremiah's Bible in the fire and mine in the toilet—sad ends for those copies of God's Word! But while men can destroy copies of God's Word, they can never destroy God's Word. The truth of this is brought out in powerful fashion by the remaining verses of Jeremiah 36. After the king burned the first scroll, the Lord said to Jeremiah: "Take yet another scroll, and write on it all the former words that were in the first scroll which Jehoiakim the king of Judah has burned" (v. 28).

Would Jeremiah be able to remember all that was in the burned scroll? Perhaps not, but the Lord has no trouble with His memory! So, the second scroll perfectly repeated the words of the first and also included "many similar words" (v. 32).

Jehoiakim paid a fearful price for casting God's Word into the fire. It caused him to experience the fire of God's judgment (v. 30). He comes to us from the Scripture he hated so much to tell us that we can't finally destroy God's Word, but it can destroy us.

What about the young men who destroyed my Bible? I don't know what became of them. They may now be out in eternity. I can only hope that they came to see the folly of their contempt for God's Word and began to treasure it.

And what about the Bible? I have a copy right here beside me.

November 8

Heavy Truth from Henry Lyte

From God's Word, the Bible...

Yet indeed I also count all things loss for the excellence of the knowledge of Christ Jesus my Lord, for whom I have suffered the loss of all things, and count them as rubbish, that I may gain Christ. . . .

Philippians 3:8

Henry Lyte was a wonderful trophy for the grace of God. Born on June 1, 1793, in Scotland, Henry entered the ministry in 1815. While engaged in ministering to others, Henry himself had not truly come to the knowledge of Christ. That would soon change. In 1816, he visited a dying priest who said that he and Henry had been wrong in not interpreting the epistles of Paul "in their plain and literal sense."

That comment prompted Henry to study the Bible more thoroughly and carefully, and that study led to his conversion.

Henry Lyte became a powerful preacher and hymn-writer. The best known of his hymns is *Abide With Me*. But he also wrote *Jesus, I My Cross Have Taken*.

This hymn has brought blessing to me. It is the hymn of one who had determined to follow the Lord no matter how great the cost. In the first verse of the hymn, Henry addresses the Lord.

Jesus, I my cross have taken,
All to leave and follow Thee;
Destitute, despised, forsaken,
Thou, from hence, my all shalt be.

In the second verse, Henry seems to speak to himself:

Perish every fond ambition,
All I've sought, and hoped, and known;
Yet how rich is my condition,
God and Christ are still my own.

It's plain that Henry scorned the notion of a cheap, easy Christianity that requires nothing and can just be tacked on to our lives as one more interest among several others. If Christianity is not the main thing to us, is it anything at all? The Lord was so important to Henry Lyte that he was willing to give up everything for Him. To those who would exclaim, "Poor Henry," he says: "Yet how rich is my condition." Those who have made Christ their all are never the worse for the bargain!

He knew how to value things. He goes on to say to God:

And, while Thou shalt smile upon me,
God of wisdom, love, and might,
Foes may hate, and friends disown me;
Show Thy face, and all is bright.

In the last verse, Henry again addresses himself:

Haste then on from grace to glory,
Armed by faith and winged by prayer;
God's eternal day's before thee,
God's own hand shall guide thee there.
Soon shall close thy earthly mission,
Swift shall pass thy pilgrim days,
Hope shall change to glad fruition,
Faith to sight, and prayer to praise.

There's so much in those lines to challenge and cheer the hearts of believers in Christ. Here's a cheerful thought: we are journeying from grace to glory. It's God grace that makes us Christians, and that grace will not finish with us until it finally deposits us in the glory of heaven.

Here's a challenging thought: we are to be "armed by faith and winged by prayer." Faith is a matter of degrees. Every Christian has faith, and every Christian needs more faith. Faith arms us. It enables us to stand strong against the devil and all his devices. And every Christian needs to be more engaged in prayer. It gives us wings. It is the way we soar aloft to the Lord in heaven.

Here's another cheerful thought: while we wait for God's eternal day to dawn, we have His guiding hand to lead us along.

And here's another challenging thought: our earthly mission shall soon close and our pilgrim days shall soon pass. We need to be about the Master's business. As wonderful as heaven will be, it will not give us the opportunity to do what we should have done while on this earth.

Henry himself got a lot of dedication to the Lord out of his life even though he was plagued with ill health for most of it. He finally entered the presence of the Lord he loved on November 20, 1847.

I'm thankful for this hymn. It makes me realize that I need to be more dedicated and determined in my service to the Lord. When this great hymn comes to mind, I invariably say this: while his name was Lyte, his hymn was heavy with truth.

November 9

Ministers and Materials

From God's Word, the Bible...

According to the grace of God which was given to me, as a wise master builder I have laid the foundation, and another builds on it. But let each one take heed how he builds on it.

1 Corinthians 3:10

Much of what Paul has to say in the early chapters of 1 Corinthians has to do with the gospel ministry. That is still his dominant emphasis in the third chapter of this epistle. He identifies Apollos and himself as "ministers" that the Lord had used to bring the Corinthians to faith in Christ (v. 5).

From that point he proceeds to picture Apollos and himself as farmers (vv. 6-8) and himself as a builder (vv. 10-17) with the church at Corinth being their field and his building (v. 9).

Paul leaves Apollos out when he, Paul, talks about himself as a builder. The reason is that Paul was the one who had laid the foundation for the church in Corinth, and he wanted to define the gospel ministry in terms of that foundation.

What was the foundation that Paul had put in place in Corinth? It was the Lord Jesus Christ (v. 10). Paul knew that other ministers would be coming into Corinth, and he wanted to warn his readers to make sure that those ministers of the future would not depart from the foundation that he himself had laid.

The true minister recognizes that it is not his job to lay a foundation for the church. That has already been done. It is now his responsibility to decide what kind of material he is going to use in building on that foundation (v. 12).

What are the materials that the minister has at his disposal? Paul pictures them as gold, silver, precious stones, wood, hay, and straw (v. 12).

It's plain that those six materials fall into two categories. The gold, silver, and precious stones are in the valuable and lasting category. The wood, hay, and straw are in the worthless and perishable category.

We must understand that Paul wasn't using these materials in a physical sense but in a spiritual sense. He was using them to picture the way the church must be built up spiritually. These materials represent the teachings or the doctrines that the minister uses to build the church. The gold, silver, and precious stones are those doctrines that best correspond to the foundation. The wood, hay, and straw represent teachings that don't correspond to the foundation.

The foundation is a gospel foundation. It consists of the redeeming work of Christ. The gold, silver, and precious stones are those teachings that set forth the work of Christ. The wood, hay, and straw are those teachings that depart from the work of Christ to offer cheap and vain substitutes.

We don't have to look very far to see that Paul's words about the ministry are just as important today as they were when he wrote them. Gold, silver, and precious stones seem to be coming from pulpits more and more infrequently. But wood, hay, and straw are being offered and heard again and again.

Where is the gold of the Lord of Glory coming to this earth in our humanity to rescue those who trust in Him from the horrible consequences of their sins? Where is the silver of His sinless life and His substitutionary death on the cross? Where are the precious stones of His resurrection from the grave and His ascension to heaven from which He poured out on His church the gift of the Holy Spirit?

Where are those preachers who preach the gospel "by the Holy Spirit sent from heaven" (1 Peter 1:12)? Where are those who feel the weight of standing before eternity-bound people? Yes, they can still be found, but they are not as numerous as they once were. In their places, we have chuckling jokesters who are more like entertainers and performers than gospel ministers.

Everyone who dares to preach should never stand before a congregation without thinking of the fearful day of exposure that is coming. Ministers and ministries will eventually be tested by the fire that "will test each one's work" to determine "of what sort it is" (v. 13).

What a sorrowful thing it will be for ministers to have revealed to the whole universe that their ministries were worthless because those ministries weren't Christ-centered! On the other hand, what a blessing it will be for ministers to finally see their Christ-centered ministries honored and rewarded (v. 14)!

Paul's words ought to cause each of us to realize how vital true gospel ministry is. If we aren't under such a ministry, we should seek it. If we are, we should prize it.

November 10

Unable and Able

From God's Word, the Bible...

"I am not able to bear all these people alone, because the burden is too heavy for me."

. . . so Christ was offered once to bear the sins of many. To those who eagerly wait for Him He will appear a second time, apart from sin, for salvation.

. . . who Himself bore our sins in His own body on the tree, that we, having died to sins, might live for righteousness—by whose stripes you were healed.

Numbers 11:14; Hebrews 9:28; 1 Peter 2:24

One of my elementary-school teachers seemed to take delight in lecturing us on the proper usage of the words "can" and "may." There was a pencil sharpener stationed on her desk, but we weren't to use it during class time without her permission. Invariably, one of my classmates would raise his or her hand and say: "Can I please use the pencil sharpener?" And our teacher would invariably respond: "I don't know. Can you?" And then she would launch into this explanation:

"'Can' is a word of ability. When you ask if you can use the pencil sharpener, you're asking if you have the ability to use it, and I think you probably do have that ability. I think you possess the ability to walk forward, insert the pencil in the sharpener, and turn the crank. The word 'may' is the word you should use. It is a word of permission. You have the ability to use the sharpener. What you're asking for is my permission."

Moses knew how to use the words "can" and "can't." In Numbers 11:14, he says to the Lord: "I am not able to bear all these people alone, because the burden is too heavy for me." He was saying: "I can't." He was saying: "I don't have the ability."

I can understand Moses' exasperation. He was in the process of leading the Israelites from crushing slavery in Egypt to freedom in their own land, the land of Canaan. One would think that those people would have been a happy, grateful lot—happy to be out of Egypt, and grateful to Moses. Someone has observed that we can go through life being humbly grateful or grumbly hateful. Many of these Israelites fell into the latter category. Instead of being thankful for the manna that the Lord provided for them, they complained and craved meat (vv. 4-6).

They were fed up with the manna, and Moses was fed up with them. They complained to Moses, and he complained to the Lord (vv. 10-15).

Moses was at his wits' end. He had reached his breaking point. That's when he essentially said to the Lord: "I can't do it any longer. I don't have the ability to put up with them any longer."

I try to never read Moses' words without thinking of the Lord Jesus Christ. The work of redemption for sinners would require Jesus to "bear" their sins. It would require Him to come to this earth in our humanity and go the cross to receive the penalty that our sins deserve. That penalty was nothing less than the wrath of God. When the Father set that work before His Son way back there in eternity past, thank God, the Son didn't say: "I can't do it." He rather said: "I can do it." And I think He also must have said: "I will do it."

So He came to this earth as a man. He lived in perfect obedience to God. He died on the cross. He arose from the grave and ascended to the Father in heaven. When it was all done, he added to His "I can" and "I will" these words: "I have." He had the ability to do the work. He was determined to do the work. And He did the work.

The main part of His saving work was His death on the cross. How very thankful we should be for that cross! There Jesus "was offered once to bear the sins of many" (Heb. 9:28). There "He Himself bore our sins in His own body" (1 Peter 2:24).

Jesus could bear our sins, and He did bear them. So we now rejoice in Him.

There was One Who was willing to die in my stead,
That a soul so unworthy might live;
And the path to the cross He was willing to tread,
All the sins of my life to forgive.

They are nailed to the cross! They are nailed to the cross!
Oh, how much He was willing to bear!
With what anguish and loss Jesus went to the cross,
But He carried my sins with Him there.
(Carrie A. Breck)

November 11

Anticipation

A Reading from Sylvia

From God's Word, the Bible...

For our citizenship is in heaven, from which we also eagerly wait for the Savior, the Lord Jesus Christ. . . .

. . .looking for the blessed hope and glorious appearing of our great God and Savior Jesus Christ. . . .

Philippians 3:20; Titus 2:13

Life is filled with much anticipation. Children look forward to Christmas with eager anticipation. Teenagers anticipate getting their driver's licenses. Even though fifty years have passed, I still remember how much Roger and I anticipated our wedding day.

One of my earliest memories involves anticipation. I was three years old. My parents were married during World War II. They lived near the naval base on the west coast where my father's ship was undergoing repairs. They were only married a few weeks until he was shipped out. Mother returned to her parents' home halfway across the country to await his return. That return never happened. He was killed a few weeks after their parting when his ship was attacked by the Japanese.

Shortly after her return home, Mother discovered she was pregnant, and I was born a few months after my father's death. Six months after I was born, my grandfather died, so Mother and I continued to live with my grandmother. Mother got a job, and Grandma took care of me when Mother was at work.

Now back to that anticipation thing. We lived a couple of miles from town. Every afternoon when it was about time for Mother to arrive home from work, Grandma would take me out to the enclosed front porch with windows on three sides. From there, we could see a long distance down the road in the direction Mother would be coming from town. I remember a small hill far in the distance. Grandma would tell me to watch for Mother's car to appear over the crest of that hill. Oh, how I would keep my eyes glued to that hill as I eagerly anticipated the sight of Mother's car! I had no doubt that she would indeed be coming over that hill.

The anticipation I felt in those childhood days is a faint picture of that which all of us who know the Lord should experience as we await His return and anticipate our heavenly home. Paul urged the Corinthians to be "eagerly waiting for the revelation of our Lord Jesus Christ" (1 Cor. 1:7).

I eagerly anticipate things I know will not be in heaven such as sin, sickness, sorrow, tears, separations, and death. None of these things will ever touch us again.

I eagerly anticipate things that must surely be part of heaven:

- Seeing the Lord Jesus Christ and worshiping Him. Every sight of His nail-scarred hands will be a reminder of the sacrifice that made heaven possible for us and will stir within us more praise and love for our Savior.
- Uncovering layer after layer of who God is and all He has done. With each discovery will come a greater depth of praise and worship.
- Discovering all the ways God protected and guided us throughout our lives when we weren't even aware of it.
- Being reunited with our believing loved ones.
- Meeting and talking with well-known saints of God, both those from the Bible and church history.
- Meeting and talking with saints of God we've never known, and hearing their stories of grace.
- Discovering all the joys God has prepared for us that we now know nothing about (1 Cor. 2:9). What are all these things God has prepared for those who love Him? I am eager to find out.

I remember the great delight and joy I felt as a three-year-old when I caught the first glimpse of Mother's car coming over the crest of that hill in the far distance. She was coming home, and I would be reunited with her! And what joy will fill our hearts when we get our first glimpse of our Lord and Savior, Jesus Christ. Whether that first glimpse comes when we enter His presence at death or when He returns to earth really doesn't matter. We will be forever in the presence of the One who loves us and gave Himself for us.

But this glorious future is only for those who belong to Christ. Those who have not repented of their sins and trusted Christ as their Lord and Savior have a future awaiting them as well—but it is not one to be eagerly anticipated. Rather it is a future to be greatly dreaded and feared.

So be sure you are in the company of those who belong to Christ, so you can eagerly anticipate the unimaginably glorious future God has prepared for those who love Him.

The Bible's Tragic Figures: Cain

FROM GOD'S WORD, THE BIBLE...

Now Cain talked with Abel his brother; and it came to pass, when they were in the field, that Cain rose up against Abel his brother and killed him.

GENESIS 4:8

The book of Genesis is the book of firsts. Adam was the first man. Eve was the first woman. Cain was the first son. Cain and Abel were the first brothers. Abel was the first man to die physically (there are other kinds of deaths). And Cain was the first hater and the first murderer. The reason Abel died is because Cain hated him and killed him.

In addition to his other "firsts," Cain was the man who engineered the first religious split. We have in Cain the beginning of a false religion. By the way, that religion is still alive and well. It is the religion of all those who believe that salvation comes to us by doing good works and not by depending completely on what God has provided in Christ.

Genesis 4 tells us that both Cain and Abel brought sacrifices to the Lord (v. 3), but the Lord wasn't pleased with Cain's. What was the difference between the two? The author of Hebrew informs us that Abel offered his sacrifice by faith or in faith, and Cain didn't (Heb. 11:4).

Faith made the difference! But what is faith? It's not, as so many seem to assume, mere positive thinking or optimism. Faith in the Bible is always believing in a message that God has revealed. The Apostle Paul writes: "So then faith comes by hearing, and hearing by the word of God" (Rom. 10:17).

We can't understand Cain and Abel if we don't go back to Genesis 3. There we have Adam and Eve falling into sin and God promising to send the Redeemer (Gen. 3:15). After making that promise, God made coverings for Adam and Eve by slaying animals (Gen. 3:21). That act was designed to show Adam and Eve something of what the Redeemer would do when He arrived on the scene. Those animals were innocent of Adam and Eve's sin, but God put them to death to cover Adam and Eve. In doing that, God was declaring that they could be fit to stand in His presence only on the basis of a substitute dying in their place. That's what the Redeemer would do. He would die as the substitute for sinners. The blood that He would shed would represent Him taking their place and receiving the penalty they deserved.

God has always had only one plan of salvation, and that plan is His Son. Sinners in the Old Testament were saved as they looked forward in faith to Christ. Sinners today are saved as they look backward in faith to Christ.

I don't hesitate to say that Adam and Eve were forgiven there in the Garden of Eden because they believed in the Redeemer that God had promised to send. They received a message from God, and they believed it. That's faith. And don't you know they also passed that message along to their sons? They would have wanted to be sure that their sons knew that they, too, must be forgiven by looking forward to the coming Christ.

Abel heard that message, believed it, and demonstrated his belief by shedding the blood of an animal just as God Himself had done in the garden of Eden. Cain, on the other hand, heard the same message. But he refused to accept it. He brought as his sacrifice some of the vegetables that he had grown. He came to God offering the work of his own hands.

We don't know how God made it clear to Cain that his sacrifice wasn't acceptable, but we know that He did. And we also know that He extended to Cain the opportunity to bring the right sacrifice (v. 7). But Cain, filled with anger and fury, refused to do what God wanted. He hated God and his way of salvation so very much that he took it out on Abel. He couldn't kill God, so he did the next best thing by killing his own brother.

On the day that Cain and Abel offered their sacrifices, the human race was divided into two streams: those who believe in God's plan of salvation and those who don't.

The message of Cain and Abel is plain. There is a way of salvation. That way is God's Son shedding His blood on the cross for sinners. We can accept it to our eternal blessing, or we can reject it to our eternal ruin. The Bible warns us about "the way of Cain" (Jude 11). That way consists of rejecting God's way.

November 13

The Bible's Tragic Figures: Esau

FROM GOD'S WORD, THE BIBLE...

And Jacob gave Esau bread and stew of lentils; then he ate and drank, arose, and went his way. Thus Esau despised his birthright.

GENESIS 25:34

The Bible presents us with many tragic figures. One of those is Esau, the grandson of Abraham and Sarah and the son of Isaac and Rebekah.

Esau had a twin brother, Jacob. But Esau was born first. That gave him something of enormous value in those days—the birthright. Among other important things, that meant he would receive a double portion of his father's inheritance.

Jacob wanted that birthright! He was probably motivated by the material wealth that it would eventually bring him.

The day came when Jacob saw his opportunity. Esau was hunting game. Jacob knew he would be famished when he returned, and he also knew very well the type of man that Esau was—the type that lives for the moment. Jacob had read his brother correctly. Esau was indeed the kind of man that wanted whatever craving he had at the moment to be satisfied in that moment.

So, Jacob had a stew ready and waiting when Esau returned. When Esau demanded some, Jacob proposed a straightforward swap—the stew for the birthright! And Esau, that man of the moment, agreed.

It seems that this deal had no actual bearing on the eventual possession of the birthright. We learn later that Isaac was still planning to bless Esau as the possessor of the birthright. That plan would cause Jacob and his mother to shift into overdrive to thwart it. But the swap of the stew for the birthright did accurately reflect the character and the priorities of Esau and Jacob.

Here is the tragedy of Esau: he was willing to trade that which was of great and lasting importance for that which was of small and temporary value. The birthright for the stew! The future for the present!

So what do we have here? Is it only an ancient story that we find to be slightly entertaining? There's much more to it than that! The truth is that Esau's bad bargain is one that has been made again and again throughout history, and it's one that is being made with incredible frequency these days.

Like Esau, we all possess something of enormous value. The Bible tells us that we aren't mere physical beings. We aren't just bodies. We are bodies and souls. And the Bible warns us to not ignore our souls. It urges us to not live for our physical needs while we ignore our greatest need, that is, the need of our souls. Jesus stated it very plainly: "For what is a man profited if he gains the whole world, and loses his own soul? Or what will a man give in exchange for his soul?" (Matt. 16:26).

Jesus also said: "Do not labor for the food which perishes, but for the food which endures to everlasting life. . . ." (John 6:27).

Jesus made the same point in his parable of the rich fool (Luke 12:13-21). The man, a farmer, was so obsessed with his crops and his barns that he gave no thought to his soul. And what did God require of him? Was it his crops or his barns? Here is the answer: "But God said to him, 'You fool! This night your soul will be required of you; then whose will those things be which you have provided?'" (v. 20).

There is only one way to properly care for our souls, and that is by committing them or entrusting them to the Lord Jesus Christ. He is the Savior.

Take care of the body? Yes, by all means. Protect it, feed it, wash it, and exercise it. But don't forget the soul. It's not a matter of choosing between caring for the body or caring for the soul. We can and should care for both, and, again, the only way to care for the soul is by trusting in what the Lord Jesus Christ came to this earth to do.

If Esau could speak audibly to us from eternity, he would plead with us to not let the passions and appetites of the moment blind us to eternal realities. Those realities may seem dim and distant now, but they will eventually become real and present to all of us—sooner perhaps than we think.

November 14

The Bible's Tragic Figures: The Elders of Israel

From God's Word, the Bible...

Then all the elders of Israel gathered together and came to Samuel at Ramah, and said to him, "Look, you are old, and your sons do not walk in your ways. Now make us a king to judge us like all the nations."

1 Samuel 8:4-5

That wonderful man of God, Samuel, was old, and the times, well, they were "a-changing." Up to this point, God had given leadership to the nation of Israel by providing them with judges (see the book of Judges). In keeping with that tradition, Samuel had appointed his sons "judges over Israel" (v. 1). We should note that this appointment came from Samuel, not from God. Samuel's two sons were nothing at all like their godly father (v. 3).

So the elders of Israel decided the time had come to take action. They wanted to end the "judge" tradition by installing a king. In their view, the time was ripe for Israel to take her place as an equal among the other nations.

There is no mention of these elders having consulted God. Had they done so, things would have been different. Had they looked into the book of Deuteronomy, they would have discovered that God didn't want Israel to be like all the other nations. He had put Israel on a pedestal from which she would have to step down in order to be like everyone else (Deut. 7:6-8; 28:9-10).

If the elders had sought the Lord's will, they would have found that He didn't want Israel to have a king at this time. Deuteronomy 17:14-20 indicates that God would give Israel a king in due time, but that time hadn't yet arrived.

Samuel's obvious displeasure (v. 6) should have been enough to derail the elders' plan for a king. Listening to Samuel had always brought blessing to the nation, and failing to listen to him had always brought trouble. But these men were so infatuated with having a king that they ignored their history.

Always a man of prayer, Samuel took the request of the elders to the Lord (v. 6). And, surprisingly, the Lord told him to give them a king. They were about to learn that it's not always a blessing when the Lord gives us what we want.

In obedience to the Lord's command, Samuel laid before the elders what they could expect from their king (vv. 9-17). At that point, they were crying for a king, but they would end up crying out because of their king (v. 18).

The warning was of no avail as these people "refused to obey the voice of Samuel" (v. 19). Their response to his words was to become even more adamant. They began by saying: "Now make us a king" (v. 5) and "Give us a king" (v. 6). They ended by saying: ". . .we will have a king. . ." (v. 19).

Why must we consider these elders of Israel to be among the Bible's tragic figures? The answer is plain. Their tragedy lay in their wanting to keep up with the times when they should have concerned themselves with keeping up with the truth. They had God's truth—there was to be no king at this time—but they willingly turned away from it. The key phrase in this situation is "like all the nations" (vv. 5,20).

Israel got their king, Saul, and they got nothing but heartache. After Saul came David, who was the king that God was planning to send them in His time. Perhaps the lesson from this episode could be put in this way: Don't settle for Saul while you wait for David.

Believers today can give into the "king thing" just as much as the elders of Samuel's time. We do so every time we set aside the truth of God in order to help the church keep up with the times. The Bible contains a straightforward message about the guilt of our sin and the holy nature of God that requires Him to judge our sin. It also plainly proclaims the judgment that God has determined, that is, eternal separation from Himself.

The Bible also declares God's gracious provision of forgiveness for sinners. That provision is Christ's death on the cross. That death consisted of Him receiving the wrath of God in the place of sinners. All who repent of their sins and trust in what Jesus did on that cross realize this precious truth: if Jesus received the wrath of God on the cross, there is no wrath left for those who receive Him.

The question ever before us is whether we will embrace the truth that God has set before us or whether we, like the elders of Israel, will set it aside so we can be considered up to date.

November 15

The Bible's Tragic Figures: King Saul

From God's Word, the Bible...

And Samuel said to Saul, "You have done foolishly. You have not kept the commandment of the Lord your God, which He commanded you. For now the Lord would have established your kingdom over Israel forever. But now your kingdom shall not continue. The Lord has sought for Himself a man after His own heart, and the Lord has commanded him to be commander over His people, because you have not kept what the Lord commanded you."

1 Samuel 13:13-14

Something was different in Israel. She now had a king. But something wasn't different. The nation was still to be governed by God's Word.

As Samuel turned the reins of leadership over to Saul, he spoke these solemn words: "Only fear the Lord and serve Him in truth with all your heart; for consider what great things He has done for you. But if you still do wickedly, both you and your king will be swept away" (12:24-25).

The success of the nation lay in both its king and people recognizing that God was their real king. It was the job of their earthly king to make sure that the nation obeyed the word of their heavenly king. If the Word of God was heard and obeyed, all would go well with the people and their king. But if they spurned God's Word, they would experience calamity. It was as simple as that.

Shortly after anointing Saul as king, Samuel made it clear to him that he would be tested on this matter of obeying God's Word. The test would come in this form—before going into battle against the Philistines, Saul would have to wait at Gilgal for seven days until Samuel came to offer a sacrifice to the Lord and to show him, Saul, what he was to do.

How was Saul to know that Samuel was telling him the truth? The very day that he warned Saul about the upcoming test, he, Samuel, gave him three detailed prophecies. Each of those prophecies came true that very day (10:1-13)! Even more confirmations would come to Saul. One was his formal selection as king by the casting of lots. That random act would seem to make it far from certain that Saul would be chosen. But the lots were cast, and his tribe was chosen, then his family, and then him (10:20-21).

Yet another confirmation was when the Lord honored Samuel's word by causing it to thunder and rain when it never thundered and rained (12:16-18).

All of these things should have made Saul say to himself: "This man Samuel speaks the Word of God which is powerful and true, and when my day of testing comes, I'm going to do as Samuel has commanded."

Saul almost made it. Six days came and went, and he waited just as Samuel had commanded. The seventh day finally dawned, the day Samuel was supposed to arrive. The hours began to tick away, and there was no Samuel. Morning came and went, as did the afternoon, and Samuel was nowhere to be seen.

Saul convinced himself that he had to act. The Philistines were gathering all around, and his people, the Israelites, were scattering. It was true that the day wasn't over, but it seemed to Saul that Samuel had failed. So instead of waiting longer, Saul offered the sacrifice. He had just finished when Samuel came strolling down the path!

Saul had failed the test. He had been told to trust God's Word, but he caved in to the pressure of the moment. Saul was called to tremble at the thought of disobeying God's Word, but he chose instead to tremble at the mustering Philistines and scattering Israelites. Because he refused to take his stand on the Word of God, Saul couldn't rightly govern the people who were called to live on the basis of that Word. So Saul's reign over Israel was doomed to fail shortly after it started.

Modern Philistines ridicule the Bible and the gospel that it presents. They ridicule the preaching of Jesus' death on the cross as the only way of salvation. We can't expect Philistines to be other than what they are. But neither should we be intimidated by them. We must not pull the plug on the doctrines of Scripture merely because the modern Philistines reject them. The fact that Philistines are gathering doesn't mean that believers in Christ should scatter.

When we find ourselves being afraid that our preaching and sharing of the gospel will make us laughingstocks, we are trembling before the Philistines.

Each child of God either trembles before this intimidating world or before God's Word (Isa. 66:2). And, like Saul, we must each decide which we will do. Saul made the wrong decision and trembled before the wrong thing. With the Lord' s help, we must make the right decision.

The Bible's Tragic Figures: Amaziah

From God's Word, the Bible...

Then Amaziah said to Amos:
"Go, you seer!
Flee to the land of Judah.
There eat bread,
And there prophesy.
But never again prophesy at Bethel,
For it is the king's sanctuary,
And it is the royal residence."

Amos 7:12-13

While Amaziah is not on the list of commonly known Bible characters, we need to know him. He is a tragic figure who emerges from the prophecy of Amos to urge us not to follow in his footsteps. What is the tragedy of Amaziah? It is that of attributing to mere men something that has come from God.

Amaziah is introduced to us as "the priest of Bethel" (v. 10). We might take that phrase to mean that he was a priest of the Lord. Amaziah was far from that. Bethel was the place where a former king of Israel, Jeroboam, had set up a false religion, one that was centered on the worship of a golden calf (1 Kings 12:28-29).

Now another Jeroboam was on the throne of Israel, and the idolatrous worship of the calf continued unabated at Bethel.

Everything seemed to be going splendidly in Israel. It was a time of prosperity and stability (Amos 3:12,15; 4:1; 6:4,6), and religion was flourishing (4:4; 5:5,21-23; 8:3,10). A nice, comfortable complacency had settled over the land.

One day Amos, a true prophet of the Lord, showed up to shatter the complacency. He declared that God was opposed to their idolatry and would shatter the idolatrous worship of Bethel (3:13-15). He also declared that the people of Israel would be carried into captivity by a foreign nation (5:2; 6:7). Amos' message was about God's wrath against sin and about judgment to come.

Amaziah was so agitated by this message that he first reported Amos to the king (7:10-11) and then confronted Amos himself (7:12-13). It's easy to see Amaziah's assumption, namely, Amos' message wasn't to be explained in terms of coming from God but rather in terms of Amos' own thinking. As far as Amaziah was concerned, Amos' message wasn't divine. It was nothing more than a mere man offering his own assessment. Since Amos' message was a mere human message, Amos could take it elsewhere. So Amaziah told the prophet to prophesy in the land of Judah but never again at Bethel (7:12-13a).

The one thing that never occurred to Amaziah was the possibility that Amos was not at Bethel by his own choice. He was there because God had sent him. And Amos' message was not his own invention. It was rather God's revelation.

Amos was quick to set Amaziah straight on these matters. He affirmed that it was God who "took" him while he was following his sheep, and it was God who plainly said to him: "Go, prophesy to My people Israel" (7:15).

This exchange between Amaziah and Amos was not merely a matter of charge and countercharge. Amos had evidence on his side. He could point to the Law of Moses that clearly declared that God would judge the idolatry of His people (Deut. 4:26-28; 6:13-15; 8:19-20; 30:17-18). Furthermore, he could point to instances in which God had visited their forefathers with judgment for going after idols, one of which was judgment for the worship of a golden calf (Ex. 32:1-6,27-28). Still further, Amos could point to things in Israel that indicated that God was already bringing the good times to an end (4:6-11).

But the evidence meant nothing to Amaziah. He was so much in love with his own world that he couldn't accept Amos' message. He looked at Bethel and saw there the king's sanctuary and his residence. It was all so marvelous, and he, Amaziah, was part of it all! He allowed it to blind him to the divine character of Amos' message, to the judgment to come on Israel, and to his own judgment (7:17).

We are confronted in the Bible with a message that claims to be from God. It's a message about our sin and about eternal judgment to come. It's also a message about the way that we can have our sins forgiven and escape coming judgment. That way is Jesus. On the basis of His perfect life and substitutionary death on the cross, guilty sinners can stand acceptably in God's presence.

Although this message is backed by abundant evidence, many dismiss it as Amaziah dismissed Amos' message. They see it as a message that men have invented. They ignore the lesson that tragic Amaziah teaches—to treat a divine message as less than divine doesn't destroy it, but rather it destroys those who reject it.

The Bible's Tragic Figures: Judas

From God's Word, the Bible...

Then Judas, His betrayer, seeing that He had been condemned, was remorseful and brought back the thirty pieces of silver to the chief priests and elders, saying, "I have sinned by betraying innocent blood." And they said, "What is that to us? You see to it!"

Matthew 27:3-4

There was actually a man who preached his own funeral service. When the time for the service came, one of his sons walked up to the pulpit and activated the playback button on a recording device. And the people heard the voice of the dearly departed. Those who knew their Bibles probably thought of that phrase in Hebrews 11:4: "he being dead yet speaks."

Judas Iscariot has been dead for many centuries, but he is also still speaking. You remember Judas. He is one of the most tragic figures in all of history. What a stained name is his! Chosen as one of Jesus' original twelve disciples, Judas turned against the Lord. For thirty pieces of silver, he arranged to have Jesus arrested. A few hours after his treacherous act, Judas threw those pieces of silver at the feet of those who had paid him and went out to hang himself.

The religious authorities, who weren't scrupulous at all about arresting, trying, and executing Jesus, were very scrupulous about the money Judas returned. It must not go into the temple treasury! That would be sacrilege! So they used it to buy a field to bury strangers in. Becoming known as "Field of Blood," it was evidently the place in which Judas killed himself.

We have the account of Judas in the Bible so we can hear that tragic man speak to us. And what does the long-dead Judas have to say? The first thing is this: *the fact that we enjoy marvelous spiritual privileges doesn't mean we have been truly saved.*

No one ever enjoyed more spiritual privileges than Judas. Jesus, the greatest of all preachers, preached the greatest of all sermons, and Judas was there to hear them. Jesus performed many miracles and all kinds of miracles, and Judas was there to see them. But with it all, Judas was an unsaved man (John 6:70-71).

We can also enjoy many spiritual privileges and still be lost. We can attend many church services, hear many sermons, read many wonderful books about the things of God, and yet never come to a true and living faith in Christ. Let us beware!

Judas also tells us that *it is crucial to accept the Lord Jesus for what He is and not for what we want Him to be.*

Have you ever wondered why Judas betrayed Jesus? The answer is bound up in the kind of kingdom that Judas was interested in. Judas wanted Jesus to set up an earthly kingdom. He, Judas, was a man of the here and now. After following Jesus for three years or so, it became apparent to him that Jesus wasn't going to do that. Some suggest that Judas decided to betray Jesus in order to force His hand. If Jesus were placed in the position of facing death, He would then use His power to defeat His enemies and establish the kingdom that Judas wanted Him to establish.

Yes, Jesus had come to this earth to set up a kingdom, but His kingdom was not to be of this earth. While Judas was out hanging himself, Jesus was speaking these words to Pontius Pilate: "My kingdom is not of this world. If my kingdom were of this world, My servants would fight, so that I should not be delivered to the Jews; but now My kingdom is not from here" (John 18:36).

The kingdom of Christ is spiritual in nature. It is set up in the hearts of sinners when the grace of God stirs them to repentance and brings them to faith in Christ. While King Jesus is now setting up His kingdom in the hearts of His people, there will come a day in which His rule will be open and obvious. On that day, every knee will bow before Him, and every tongue will confess that He is the King of Kings and the Lord of Lords (Phil. 2:9-11; Rev. 19:16).

But many, like Judas, aren't interested in that kind of kingdom. They would rather have a Christ who helps them in this world instead of preparing them to enter the next world. Meanwhile, they fail to see that nothing helps us more in this life than the confidence that we are ready for the life to come.

The still-speaking Judas urges us not to repeat his thinking and his doing. Are we willing to listen to him?

November 18

The Hymn of the Three C's

From God's Word, the Bible...

"To whom then will you liken Me,
Or to whom shall I be equal?" says the Holy One.

Isaiah 40:25

What are the most treasured and well-liked of all the hymns? Every list I have seen includes *How Great Thou Art*. Others, as you might suppose, are *Amazing Grace, The Old Rugged Cross, Holy, Holy, Holy* and *Blessed Assurance*.

How Great Thou Art came to us down a winding road. It went from Sweden to Germany to Russia before coming to the United Kingdom and America.

It was written by Carl Gustav Boberg in Monsteras, Sweden, in 1885. One Sunday afternoon, twenty-six-year-old Boberg was making his way home from the church that he served as pastor when he was caught in a terrific thunderstorm. After finding shelter, Boberg marveled at the power of the storm. When it passed, Boberg took notice of the beautiful rainbow and the happy singing of the birds. It all made such a profound impression on him that he took up his pen and poured out adoration and worship to God. The hymn was eventually translated from Russian to English by missionary Stuart Hine in 1949. It was greatly popularized by George Beverly Shea and Cliff Barrows in the Billy Graham crusades.

It's the hymn of the Three "C's," taking us from creation to the cross to the culmination of all things. The marvel of God's creation is set forth in the first two verses:

O Lord my God! When I in awesome wonder
Consider all the works Thy hand hath made.
I see the stars, I hear the rolling thunder,
Thy power throughout the universe displayed.

When through the woods and forest glades I wander
And hear the birds sing sweetly in the trees;
When I look down from lofty mountain grandeur
And hear the brook and feel the gentle breeze.

With these things in place, the refrain is inevitable. It is a burst of triumphant praise:

Then sings my soul, my Savior God, to Thee:
How great Thou art, how great Thou art!
Then sings my soul, my Savior God, to Thee:
How great Thou art, how great Thou art!

The hymn takes us to the cross in these moving words:

And when I think that God, His Son not sparing,
Sent Him to die, I scarce can take it in;
That on the cross, my burden gladly bearing,
He bled and died to take away my sin.

That verse, of course, also calls for the same triumphant burst of praise in the refrain as the verses about God's creative wonders. Does the cross of Christ fill us with adoring wonder? If it doesn't we should ponder deeply the gap between our "burden" and the "gladly bearing." Our burden was our sin that justly deserved the wrath of God. On the cross, Jesus not only took that burden, but also took it willingly and gladly. Can it be? Jesus gladly took the burden of my sin and judgment so I don't have to carry that burden any longer! Let me realize this to the point that I can sing, "Then sings my soul. . . ."

Then there's that great verse of culmination:

When Christ shall come with shout of acclamation
And take me home, what joy shall fill my heart!
Then I shall bow in humble adoration,
And there proclaim, my God, how great Thou art!

That verse also leads quite inevitably to the refrain. Perhaps there has never been a more happy marriage between verses and refrain than the one we find in this superb hymn.

In my estimation, the church needs to sing this hymn and sing it often. The reason is that she, the church, is starved for a sense of the greatness of God. The problem isn't that God is withholding the evidences of His greatness from us. It's rather that we are depriving ourselves of His greatness by our fascination with little things. Pastors and church-goers seem to take enormous delight in the troubleshooter God who concerns Himself with helping us cope with the aggravations, frustrations, and irritations that crop up in daily living. Our need is to lift our eyes from our little living to see the wonders of the creation, the cross, and the culmination until we join Boberg in boisterously singing to the Lord: "How great Thou art!"

November 19

An Old Man with a Flat Tire

From God's Word, the Bible...

O God, You have taught me from my youth;
And to this day I declare Your wondrous works.
Now also when I am old and grayheaded,
O God, do not forsake me,
Until I declare Your strength to this generation,
Your power to everyone who is to come.

Psalm 71:17-18

I don't think of myself as old, but I sometimes get reminded in a jolting sort of way that I am. Sylvia and I were returning from a church service one night when our car warned us that we were losing air in one of our rear tires. We pulled into a convenience store parking lot to take a look. The problem was easy to see. A steel rod had gone through one side of the tire and had come out the other side. The tire was now completely flat.

I immediately ran into a problem. There was a lever that had to be pulled to release the spare tire, but it was tucked so neatly away that I was having a hard time locating it. The woman who was working in the convenience store came to my rescue. She knew a man inside the store who would be willing to help. Out he came, and in mere minutes had the tire changed.

It was when I offered to pay him something for helping that I received my jolt. He refused with these words: "I never take money from an old man that needs help."

Then and there I knew—in blunt and brutal fashion—I am an old man. These words from David quickly sprang to my mind:

I have been young, and now am old. . . .
(Ps. 37:25a)

I find as I advance in years that I can relate very easily to the picture of old age in the opening verses of Ecclesiastes 12:

- the keepers of the house tremble;
- the strong men bow down;
- the grinders cease because they are few;
- those that look through the windows grow dim;
- the doors are shut in the streets;

- the daughters of music are brought low;
- the almond tree blossoms.

These descriptive phrases relate to the hands, the legs, the teeth, the eyes, the ears, the voice, and the hair (which turns white, or in my case, loose). I can especially identify with this part of old age—"one rises up at the sound of a bird." That is the author's way of depicting the old person being easily awakened from sleep. I know what it is to wake up at the sound of a bird—and it doesn't have to be a very big bird.

Ecclesiastes 12:5 humorously adds another detail of old age: "The grasshopper is a burden." If a grasshopper should land on the shoulder of an old person, it would seem to be a heavy load. The same verse also tells us that "desire fails," that is, the old person isn't interested in doing things that used to fire his interest.

This passage is depressing if we forget to lay the blessings of old age alongside the burdens. And old age does have its blessings. I try to keep in mind that I could have died at a very young age (I had a couple of close calls) and been deprived of many years of happiness and satisfaction.

As the years slide by—ever more rapidly it seems—I also try to remind myself to look forward to heaven. We Christians are supposed to know that this world isn't our home. We are pilgrims who are traveling through this world to our true home in heaven. But if we're not careful we can get so attached to this world that we're not looking forward to heaven. Matthew Henry cautions us that the world is a traveling place, not a stopping place. We need that caution.

I would like to see more yearning for heaven. In my years as a pastor I detected an attitude among many believers that could be put like this: "If I have to leave this world, I guess heaven is better than the other place."

Heaven will not just be better than "the other place." It's going to be great! Let's keep reminding ourselves of that and coach ourselves to look forward to it.

I also want to use my older years to be ever more grateful to the Lord Jesus for His redeeming work on my behalf. He is my way to heaven.

I'm grateful to the man who changed my tire. I'm also grateful that he called me an old man. It made me think about old age, and I realized that it's not bad to be old.

November 20

Dr. Brown's Body

From God's Word, the Bible...

But someone will say, "How are the dead raised up?
And with what body do they come?"

1 Corinthians 15:35

I was the guest preacher. The Sunday evening worship service began with the congregation singing a hymn. After that a gentleman came to the pulpit to share this announcement: "It is my sad responsibility to inform you that Dr. Brown passed away this afternoon."

Dr. Brown had been retired for a long time after being the pastor of that church for close to thirty years. He had served with distinction and was widely and highly esteemed.

Since Dr. Brown had been ill for quite some time, I wasn't surprised to hear that he had died. I was surprised to hear the next words from the man who was making the announcement. He said: "Dr. Brown has already received that new body that the Bible promises."

The Christian will definitely receive a new body. There should be no doubt about that. But the Christian doesn't receive his new body when he dies. That comes later.

When the believer dies, a separation takes place. The soul is separated from the body, and the soul goes immediately into the presence of God. The Apostle Paul describes the believer's death as being "absent from the body" and being "present with the Lord" (2 Cor. 5:8). It's certainly correct to say that a believer goes to heaven when he dies, but that is true of the soul only.

What happens to the body of the believer? Generally speaking, it goes into the grave. So, when the believer dies his soul goes to heaven and his body goes to the grave.

Is that the final word for the body? No, not at all! The body will eventually be raised from the grave and will be reunited with the soul. But that won't happen until Jesus comes again. That's when Dr. Brown will get his new body, but not until then.

The souls of dead believers are at perfect peace with the Lord, but they also yearn for that day when they will be reunited with their bodies. We might say they are now happy but incomplete. Their condition could be pictured in terms of a young couple who are engaged to be married. They are happy during their engagement, but they aren't complete. And they eagerly look forward to their wedding day when they will be complete.

The resurrection of the body and the reunion of it with the soul is "the blessed hope" of the Christian (Titus 2:13). Then the Christian will be complete.

After hearing me preach on the resurrection of the Christian's body, a lady angrily confronted me after the service with this question: "Why would we want these old bodies back?"

She was assuming that the resurrection of the body means getting this body back as it is now. It was evident that she had not read with understanding the teaching of Paul in 1 Corinthians 15. The Apostle says there's a sense in which Christians will get their bodies back. Those bodies that go into the graves will come out of the graves. But the bodies that come out of those graves will surpass those that go into it, just as plants that spring from the ground far surpass the seeds that go into the ground.

Paul informs us that these bodies are "sown in corruption," that is, they are subject to decay and deterioration, but the bodies that are raised from the graves will be "incorruptible" (v. 42). Further, these bodies are "sown in dishonor" (v. 3). There is no dignity or honor in death! But when Jesus comes to raise His people, the dishonor will be gone as our new bodies are clothed in glory. Still further, Paul tells us that these bodies are "natural" (v. 44). They were made for this natural realm and are suited for it, but when Jesus comes, they will be raised and suited to the eternal world.

While we don't have all the answers that we might desire about the nature of the resurrected bodies of believers, it should be enough for us to know that those bodies will be modeled and fashioned after the resurrection body the Lord Jesus has (vv. 45-49; 1 John 3:2).

It was my privilege to know Dr. Brown. He was a good and godly man. His soul is now with the Lord, and his body is in the grave. If his body lying there in the grave could hear, I would say: "Wait a little longer. Glory is coming!"

November 21

Pushing the Pool or Moving the Bucket

FROM GOD'S WORD, THE BIBLE...

If we confess our sins, He is faithful and just to forgive us our sins and to cleanse us from all unrighteousness.

1 JOHN 1:9

Our grandchildren were playing in one of those inflatable pools. You know the kind. Fill it with air and put water in it, and, presto, you have a swimming pool. It took a lot of water to fill this pool, so much so that it was very heavy and impossible to move around.

The children also had water guns that could shoot a stream of water for an impressive distance. One of their favorite games was to sit in the pool with those guns while they tried to shoot water into a bucket a few feet from the pool. But there was a problem. They had stationed the bucket so far away that they were having trouble hitting it. Our grandson, Isaiah, came up with a solution. He asked his dad to move the pool closer to the bucket!

It occurred to me that I have often been guilty of trying to do the very thing that Isaiah suggested, that is, to move the pool when it would have been much easier to move the bucket.

The Christian life is hard. The Bible never hides that fact. It likens it to carrying a cross (Matt. 16:24). That's hard. It also pictures the Christian as a soldier in a war, an athlete competing in a race, and a farmer trying to raise a crop (2 Tim. 2:3-6). Each of those professions requires diligent, devoted effort, and each involves danger of some kind. Those who suggest that there is a formula for taking the difficulty out of Christian living simply don't know what they're talking about.

Because Christian living is so difficult in and of itself, the very last thing we need to do is to make it more difficult. The difficulty that the Lord has put in it should be enough for us without adding difficulties of our own. That's what the devil would like for us to do. He wants us to rise from our beds each morning and start shoving on a very heavy pool instead of moving the bucket.

What pool does the devil have you shoving around? Is it guilt? That's an impossibly heavy pool to shove around!

King David knew about guilt. He had done terrible things, committing adultery with Bathsheba, having her husband murdered, and then trying to cover it all up. For a long time, he lived with horrible guilt. He speaks of "groaning all the day long" (Ps. 32:3).

Here in David's own words is how he found relief:

I acknowledged my sin to You,
And my iniquity I have not hidden,
I said, "I will confess my transgressions to the Lord,"
And You forgave the iniquity of my sin.
(Ps. 32:5)

David's relief came when he repented of his sins, and he is quick to assure us that all of God's people can find relief from their guilt in the same way:

For this cause everyone who is godly shall pray to You. . . .
(Ps. 32:6a)

Repentance is turning from our sins to God. To turn toward something, we have to turn away from something. To turn toward God, we have turn away from sin. We have to do an about face. Before we repent, our faces are toward sin and our backs toward God. When we repent we turn our backs toward our sins and our faces toward God.

If we're living with the heaviness of guilt, we must repent! The Lord gives marvelous assurances to all who sincerely repent. In regard to sins of which we repent, the Lord promises:

- to remove them from us as far as the east is from the west (Ps. 103:12);
- to pass over them (Micah 6:18);
- to cast them into the depths of the sea (Micah 7:19);
- to put them behind His back (Isa. 38:17);
- to blot them out (Isa 44:22);
- to remember them no more (Jer. 31:34);
- to make them impossible to find (Jer. 50:20).

Repentance itself is not an easy thing. We must have grace from God to do it. Let's ask God for that grace, and let's always remember that repentance is much less difficult than living daily with crushing guilt. The yoke of Christ is light compared to that of sin (Matt. 11:28-30). We might say that repentance, as difficult as it is, is like moving a bucket. Living with guilt is like trying to push a pool. So let's move the bucket.

November 22

From Riches to Poverty to Riches

A Reading from Sylvia

From God's Word, the Bible...

For you know the grace of our Lord Jesus Christ, that though He was rich, yet for your sakes He became poor, that you through His poverty might become rich.

2 Corinthians 8:9

In the mid to late 1940s, my mother and I were living with my widowed grandmother. My mother was also a widow, my father having been killed in World War II before I was born. Mother was a career woman with a good job that she enjoyed. She wore nice clothes and shoes. My grandmother's house was nicer than most homes in our small community. Mother had paid to have a bathroom installed, which was a luxury few homes in our community had. Grandma took care of me while Mother was at work. So life was good, comfortable, and quite easygoing for Mother.

And then she met Gene Miller, a poor, struggling farmer. After a brief courtship they were married, and Mother's life drastically changed. She quit her job, and we moved to a farm seventeen miles from town. My new dad didn't own the farm; he just rented the land and the small four-room house that came with it.

The house had no electricity, no running water, and, of course, no bathroom. It was located two miles from the highway, and before the road reached our house it changed from a gravel road to a dirt road. That meant when it rained, the dirt road became a mud road and sometimes so impassable that we had to leave our car at the end of the gravel road and walk through the mud the last quarter of a mile to our house.

Why did my mother give up the easy life she had in exchange for a difficult life as the wife of a poor farmer? It was love. She loved Dad enough to become poor with him.

The Lord Jesus Christ did a similar thing for us, but on a much greater scale. He left the beauty, glory, and riches of heaven to come to this earth in our humanity. His life of perfect obedience to the Father was marked by poverty and difficulty (Matt. 8:20). Then He died on the cross a death like no one else has ever died, taking upon Himself our sins and receiving the full fury of God's wrath against those sins.

And why did He do it? It was love. He loved us enough to lay aside the riches He enjoyed in heaven and become poor, so that we who were poor in our sins and hopelessness could become rich. No, this isn't referring to monetary riches, but to the greater riches that are ours as believers in Christ: forgiveness of sins, right standing with God, and an eternal home in heaven.

What was the result of Christ's willingness to come to this earth to carry out the plan of redemption? A multitude of people who were poor in their sins and living under the judgment of God have become rich.

And what were the results of my mother's willingness to marry Gene Miller? After a few months we got electricity in that little house and a pump at the kitchen sink to bring in cold water. Four years later, Mom and Dad were able to purchase a farm of their own closer to town. It had a large farmhouse that Dad turned into a comfortable home where Mom lived until her death. As a result of the choice Mom made, she and I both became rich. No, not monetarily, but in much better ways. Mother acquired a husband who loved her devotedly the rest of her life. I acquired a wonderful Christian father who couldn't have loved me more if I had been his own flesh and blood. God blessed their marriage with four sons who adored their mom, and my life was enriched by growing up with siblings.

I am so thankful that Mother chose to lay aside her comfortable life and financial stability to become poor for a season so that she and I could become rich in many ways. And oh, how much more thankful I am that the Lord Jesus Christ chose to lay aside His riches and become poor for a season to enrich me with His glorious salvation.

November 23

Simple Song, Sublime Truth

FROM GOD'S WORD, THE BIBLE...

Blessed is he whose transgression is forgiven,
Whose sin is covered.

PSALM 32:1

Too great a sinner to be saved! That's what Walter "Happy Mac" MacDonald thought many years ago. Although he had built a reputation for himself as a dancer, his sinful living had made him miserable. One evening in the early 1930s he made his way into a meeting of the Pacific Garden Mission in Chicago and heard the gospel. Although the workers there urged him to turn to Christ, he refused. But he kept attending the services.

Walter and Ethelwyn Taylor, known as Pa and Ma Taylor, were leading this mission effort. Ma Taylor carried a special burden for Happy Mac and prayed for his salvation. When he finally came for counseling, he poured out to the Lord these sorrowful words: "You don't know how bad I am, Lord. Really, I'm the worst man in the world. You can't save me; I'm too bad."

Upon hearing that prayer, Ma Taylor recalled some words she had recently heard from a preacher. This preacher, Percy Crawford, had been a very sinful young man, but he turned to the Lord. In relating his conversion, Crawford said: "Calvary covers it all." Ma shared those words with Happy Mac, who immediately embraced them and trusted Christ.

Soon after that Ma Taylor wrote these words:

Far dearer than all that the world can impart
Was the message that came to my heart;
How that Jesus alone
For my sin did atone,
And Calvary covers it all.

Chorus:
Calvary covers it all,
My past with its sin and stain;
My guilt and despair
Jesus took on Him there,
And Calvary covers it all.

This is a simple song, consisting of short, plain words, the longest of which has ten letters. That word is "redemption," which appears in this verse:

How matchless the grace, when I looked on the face
Of this Jesus, my crucified Lord;
My redemption complete
I then found at His feet,
And Calvary covers it all.

Here is the sublime truth of Ma Taylor's simple hymn: Calvary covers it all! Are you a big sinner? Jesus is a bigger Savior than you are a sinner!

What is sin? It is refusing to live the way that God requires. God has given us certain commandments by which He expects us to live. Look at the Ten Commandments in Exodus 20:1-17. Each one of those commandments testifies against us. Not one of us has perfectly kept them, and each broken commandment shouts the word "Sinner" at us.

The problem with being sinners is that we eventually have to come before the God who gave these commandments. If we stand before Him in our sins, He will drive us from His presence into everlasting ruin. But if those sins are covered, hidden from His view, He will receive us.

Jesus' death on the cross provides the covering we need. He received the penalty for sinners so all who trust in Him will not receive that penalty themselves. Because of what Jesus did on the cross, God throws a cover over our sins so He can no longer see them. Sin covered so that it can no longer be seen—what a blessed thought! And it's Jesus' death on the cross of Calvary that provides the cover.

The Ark of the Covenant in the Old Testament pictures this. The Ten Commandments were placed in the lower part of the Ark. Above those commandments was the Mercy Seat where the High Priest sprinkled the blood of the sacrifice. The Mercy Seat was exactly the same width as the box that contained the commandments. The Ark, then, gave this testimony: the blood of the atonement was sufficient to cover the broken commandments.

Those who trust Christ, no matter how sinful they have been, are saved and can now sing:

How blessed the thought, that my soul by Him bought,
Shall be His in the glory on high;
Where with gladness and song
I'll be one of the throng,
And Calvary covers it all.

November 24

I Am Resolved

From God's Word, the Bible…

Therefore, whether you eat or drink, or whatever you do, do all to the glory of God.

1 Corinthians 10:31

Determination, not desire, is the key to spiritual attainment. Many of us desire to progress in spirituality. The problem is that we're not determined to progress.

A great example of determination is Jonathan Edwards. Before he was twenty years of age, he wrote seventy resolutions to guide and govern his spiritual life. These resolutions can easily be found online.

We often assume that we can't expect young people to be concerned about growing in grace and in the knowledge of the Lord. We tend to think God has a cheaper, easier brand of Christianity for them and doesn't expect much out of them until they are adults.

Edwards thought differently. If one's youthful years aren't too early to be saved by Christ from eternal woe, they surely aren't too early to give to the Lord a heart of love and to plan for a life of devotion. If one is saved from a very serious situation, such a person should be very serious about the Lord.

Edwards' resolutions throb with a seriousness that puts most of us to shame. Ours seems to be a time in which it's never possible to be too lighthearted and casual about Christianity, but it's always possible to be too serious about it.

Edwards' resolutions suggest to me a threefold division—the preeminent, the prominent and the prudent.

With the word *preeminent*, I'm referring to the priority of his life, which was living for the glory of God. It's very significant that the first resolution begins: "I will do whatsoever I think to be most to the glory of God. . . ."

What is it to live for the glory of God? It's to live in such a way that the credit for our lives goes to God. It's to live in such a way that others will have to note that there are higher principles at work, and that those principles come, not from within ourselves, but from God.

Many regard this kind of living as detrimental to happiness. Edwards didn't. In his first resolution, he inserts the words "my own good, profit, and pleasure" immediately after "the glory of God." As far as he was concerned, the two were one and the same—living for God's glory and experiencing happiness. Holiness doesn't destroy our happiness; it secures it. Edwards wanted to be happy here, but he also wanted to live in such a way as to obtain "much happiness in the other world" (Resolution #22).

With the word *prominent*, I'm referring to those realities of which he was always conscious—realities that drove him to make God his priority.

Death is one of those realities. Edwards often reminds himself to live with death in mind. In one resolution, he reminds himself to "think much, on all occasions, of my dying." The awareness of death, of course, should bring with it the awareness of our accountability to God for how we have lived. With Edwards, death and judgment were inseparably linked.

Edwards' also lived with the ongoing awareness of how very inclined we are to sin and how very necessary it is for us to concern ourselves with "the state" of our souls. Resolution #48 reads: "Resolved, constantly, with the utmost niceness and diligence, and the strictest scrutiny, to be looking into the state of my soul, that I may know whether I have truly an interest in Christ or no; that when I come to die, I may not have any negligence respecting this to repent of."

If we want to achieve a higher level of spirituality, we would do well to think frequently, as Edwards did, about death, judgment, sin, and the state of our souls.

With the word *prudent*, I'm referring to the practical steps he took. We should note that his concern for holy living extended to every aspect of life, including usage of time, treatment of animals, assurance, prayer, faithfulness, speaking, the Lord's Day, eating and drinking, respect for parents, general attitudes, and afflictions.

All of Edwards' resolutions search me, but none more than these:

- "To strive every week to be brought higher in religion, and to a higher exercise of grace, than I was the week before" (#30);
- To never ". . .act as if I were any way my own, but entirely and altogether God's. . ." (#43);
- To live in such a way as to have "Christianity always shining in its true lustre" (#63).

Can we do as well as Edwards did? Probably not. Can we do better than we are doing? Yes. And the first step in doing better must surely be to think long and hard about what the Lord Jesus has done for us. In heaven's glory, He thought of us; God the Father and Jesus resolved that He would come into this world to live a perfect life and die a sacrificial death for sinners, and then rise again in justification of all who would trust Him. Such was His resolution for us; are we resolved to live for Him and His glory?

The Voice of Christ

From God's Word, the Bible...

"Most assuredly, I say to you, he who hears My word and believes in Him who sent Me has everlasting life, and shall not come into judgment, but has passed from death into life."

John 5:24

The words of our verse occur in the midst of a section that stresses the voice of Christ. The word "hear" appears four times in this section (vv. 24-29), while the word "voice" appears twice and "word" appears once.

Ours is a time of voices competing for our attention and allegiance. The voices of pleasure, possessions, politics, and position speak to us in alluring tones. The voice of Christ often seems to be drowned out by the other voices, but it is still sounding, and, like the others, it also calls for our allegiance.

Why should we give priority to hearing the voice of Christ? First, *it is the voice of absolute authority.*

The authority of Jesus is the central issue in John 5. The chapter begins with Jesus healing a man who had been lame for thirty-eight years (vv. 1-9). This would seem to have caused great rejoicing, but there was a fly in the ointment. Jesus healed this man on the Sabbath (v. 9). The religious leaders of the Jews were so incensed over Jesus doing this that they actually sought to kill Him (v. 16).

Jesus added fuel to the fire by claiming that this miracle was the result of Him and God the Father working together (v. 17). The religious leaders understood what Jesus was saying. He was claiming to be equal with God (v. 18). They were right.

Beginning in verse 19, Jesus defended His claim by saying three times "Most assuredly, I say to you. . ." (vv. 19,24,25). Jesus used this phrase when He wanted to call attention to something of tremendous importance. John's Gospel relates twelve such occasions.

These words are, in and of themselves, a claim of authority. When we want to establish our authority for saying something, we quote experts in that field. But there was no higher authority for Jesus to quote. So when He was dealing with something that required authority, He merely said: "I say to you."

We see Him doing this in the Sermon on the Mount. Several times He indicated what the religious leaders were teaching the people and then corrected each of those teachings with these words: "But I say to you" (Matt. 5:17-48). Those who heard Him noted His authority (Matt. 7:29).

We should understand that Jesus' authority was also substantiated by the witness of John the Baptist (vv. 31-35), by the miracles that He performed (v. 36), and by God the Father Himself (v. 37).

All of these evidences for Jesus converge in a mighty way to tell us that we should listen to His voice. It is the voice of authority.

A second reason for us to listen to the voice of Christ is this: *it is the voice that announces wonderful news.*

Jesus says: ". . . he who hears My word and believes in Him who sent Me has everlasting life. . ." (v. 24).

Wonderful news indeed! All who believe in Jesus have everlasting life! Jesus doesn't say: "he who is rich," or "he who is very intelligent," or "he who enjoys fame and status." No, He says, ". . . he who hears My voice and believes in Him who sent Me." That is the person who receives everlasting life.

Hearing and believing! How can we hear the word of Jesus? We can hear it by reading the Bible and by listening to the preaching and teaching of the Bible. That is where the Lord Jesus speaks. We must hear before we can believe. Paul writes: "So then faith comes by hearing, and hearing by the word of God" (Rom. 10:17).

What is it to believe? It's not just knowing the facts about the Lord Jesus and believing those facts to be true. It is a matter of committing ourselves to Him as the only possible way for our sins to be forgiven.

There's yet another reason we should pay close attention to the voice of Christ. *It is the voice that announces what happens to those who refuse to believe*. Those who refuse Christ "come into judgment" (v. 24).

Jesus is the bridge or the passageway from the land of condemnation into the land of life. Those who refuse to heed His voice and use Him as their bridge must remain in condemnation. To have life, we must have Jesus, and to have Jesus we must hear His voice and believe in Him (John 3:18,36; 14:6; 1 John 5:12).

Have you heard the voice of Jesus in His Word, the Bible, and are you trusting Him alone for your salvation?

The Word and Prayer

FROM GOD'S WORD, THE BIBLE...

And take the helmet of salvation, and the sword of the Spirit, which is the word of God; praying always with all prayer and supplication in the Spirit, being watchful to this end with all perseverance and supplication for all the saints.

EPHESIANS 6:17-18

The church is engaged in spiritual warfare. This stems from her having an enemy—Satan. While he can roar like a lion (1 Peter 5:8), Satan often prefers to do his work by relying on his ability to deceive. He is so effective with this strategy that Paul repeatedly warns his readers to not be deceived (1 Cor. 3:18; 15:33; Gal. 6:7; Eph 5:6; 2 Thess. 2:3).

To fight Satan and his forces we must put on the armor of God. The following parts of the armor are defensive in nature: the girdle of truth (v. 14a), the breastplate of righteousness (v. 14b), the feet shod with the preparation of the gospel of peace (v. 15), the shield of faith (v. 16) and the helmet of salvation (v. 17a).

After listing those items, Paul proceeds to call attention to the weapon that Christians have been given, namely, "the sword of the Spirit which is the word of God" (Eph. 6:17b). The Word of God is for both defense and offense. By relying on its teachings, we can fend off Satan's attack. By wielding it in proclamation, we can put him and his forces to flight. The reason is the Word of God is a very powerful weapon (Heb. 4:12).

When the church as a whole employs this weapon, she will see Satan's strongholds or fortifications fall. And the arguments Satan plants in sinners, arguments that they use to exalt themselves against the knowledge of God, will be cast down. Through the power of the Word of God, the church can expect to see such sinners captured and brought into obedience of Christ (2 Cor. 10:4-5).

It is interesting that Paul wraps up his description of the Christian's armor by calling his readers to pray "always with all prayer and supplication in the Spirit" (v. 18).

Some have wondered why he didn't include prayer as part of the armor. The reason may very well be that he wanted to emphasize that each part of the armor is to be taken up and employed with prayer.

Prayer isn't to be the casual, nonchalant muttering of words. It must be sincere and fervent. We must not be casual about war! Warfare praying requires certain things. First, we are to use "all prayer," that is, every form of prayer. Prayers of thanksgiving, supplication or petition, and intercession all play a vital role in our combat against Satan, as do public and private praying. The Apostle especially calls for supplication as the key form of praying. We cannot succeed in our warfare apart from prayer that beseeches God to supply the strength and resolve we so profoundly need.

Then all this praying must be done "always." We are to "pray without ceasing" (1 Thess. 5:17). This doesn't mean that we're to do nothing but pray. That's impossible because Scripture clearly assigns us other responsibilities. But whatever we do is to be done with an attitude of prayer and a readiness to resort to prayer.

All of this is to be done "in the Spirit." We are to recognize our weakness apart from God, and we are to depend on the Spirit to give us the spirit of prayer, to help us formulate our petitions, and to give us the warmth of spirit and the fervency that prayer requires.

How the teaching of the apostle challenges and rebukes us! Most Christians have much to lament here. Our praying is often spasmodic, half-hearted, and haphazard. We're engaged in a most fearful warfare with a dreadful adversary, but we're also assured that our God occupies a throne of grace and that we can, through prayer, come there and "obtain mercy and find grace to help in time of need" (Heb. 4:16).

From time to time we hear accounts of individuals living as paupers while they have a fortune laid aside. We shake our heads in wonderment at such accounts. But many Christians are doing something very similar in the spiritual realm as they fail to draw help from the throne of grace through the privilege of prayer.

The church has always made her greatest advances when she most vigorously gave herself to prayer. Satan is not impressed with our personalities and our programs. But when the church prays, the earth trembles beneath her and Satan flees.

How blessed we are to have the Word of God and prayer! How foolish we are to not make better use of them!

November 27

Living a "Ful"er Life (1)

From God's Word, the Bible...

. . .in everything give thanks; for this is the will of God in Christ Jesus for you.

1 Thessalonians 5:18

The older I get, the more I realize how quickly this life is passing. I realize that it will soon be over, and I will be out in eternity. This makes me think about how I want to spend the rest of my days. First, I want to be *more thankful*. Every Christian can easily make a list of things he or she is thankful for—family, health, the beauties of creation, material possessions, as well as many other things. While we give thanks to the Lord for such things, we should be striving to be more conscious of them and more abundant in our praise.

There is, of course, one blessing that surpasses all others. The Apostle Paul says: "Thanks be to God for His indescribable gift" (2 Cor. 9:15).

Of all the gifts that God so generously gives, only one can be called "indescribable." That is the gift of His Son. That best-loved of all Bible verses, John 3:16, says: "For God so loved the world that He gave His only begotten Son that whoever believes in Him should not perish but have everlasting life."

Christians are very familiar with those words, and most would quickly agree that Christ is the best of all God's gifts. But even Christians can fail to realize just how grand that gift is. We know Jesus came to this earth as a man and that He died on the cross, but we don't always realize the true meaning of His death. Some admit that they don't understand how Jesus dying on a cross could provide salvation for us. The problem is that they are thinking of His death in physical terms only. We must never do that. Lots of men died on lots of crosses in those days, but Jesus' death was special. He received in the space of the six hours that He was on the cross the eternal wrath that our sins deserve. Because He was God in human flesh, He could receive that amount of wrath in that length of time.

When we truly understand what Jesus went through on that cross, we find it much easier to be more thankful. I don't want a day to go by without reflecting deeply on that cross, and, as I reflect, I want to pray the words of Fanny J. Crosby:

Let me love Thee more and more,
'Till this fleeting, fleeting life is o'er;

'Till my soul is lost in love,
In a brighter, brighter world above.
May Thy tender love to me
Bind me closer, closer, Lord, to Thee.

I also want to be more thankful for great public worship. Nothing so feeds and nourishes the soul as God-honoring, Christ-centered, Spirit-anointed worship. Alas, it seems to be harder and harder to find.

Good worship requires good preaching. I would like to hear preaching that is so anointed by the Spirit of God that I am, in the words of Charles Wesley, "lost in wonder, love and praise."

Preaching has been in a state of decline for several years. This isn't exactly a new thing. Centuries ago, John Calvin offered this lament:

> At the present day there are many who are well-nigh sickened by the very name of preaching, because there are so many stupid, ignorant men who blurt out their worthless brainwaves from the pulpit.[8]

But there have also been eras of powerful preaching. Oh, to see such an era again!

Good worship also requires robust congregational singing. To me, loud, boisterous, triumphant, and happy congregational singing is one of the finest things on this side of heaven. Such singing can lift the spirits of sad saints, and it can convince unbelievers that Christianity is a wonderful thing.

Still further, good worship requires consciousness of being in the presence of the majestic, glorious and holy God. Oftentimes "worship services" seem to be more devoted to entertaining the hearers and cultivating an air of lightheartedness and frivolity than they are to standing in awe of God. My wife and I are thankful to be members of a church that truly seeks to honor the Lord.

As life continues to pass, I'm coaching myself to making it "ful"-er, and the first of my "fuls" is thankful—thankful for all of God's blessings, but especially for the salvation provided by Christ and for worship that truly honors Him.

8 Cited by Tom Lyon, "The Centrality of Preaching," *Banner of Truth Magazine*, November, 2005, p. 10

November 28

Living a "Ful"er Life (2)

From God's Word, the Bible...

Finally then, brethren, we urge and exhort in the Lord Jesus that you should abound more and more, just as you received from us how you ought to walk and to please God. . . .

1 Thessalonians 4:1

I want in the days that I have remaining to be more thankful. I also want to be *more prayerful*. Prayer is amazing to me. I can speak here on earth and be heard in heaven by the God who made all things and rules over all things to His eternal glory.

When I pray, I'm heard in heaven by the gracious God who planned my salvation, and by the Lord Jesus who purchased it for me on the cross. Heard in heaven! What a privilege! And what a God! Out of all the prayers that ascend to Him, He hears mine as if it were the only one being offered.

The amazing nature of prayer invariably makes me think of another amazing thing, namely, that I don't pray more than I do! To have the ear of God and not avail myself of it! What utter folly!

I've prayed all through my years, but never as much and never as well as I should have. In my older years, I want to do better. I want to be often at my Father's throne, offering adoration and praise, confessing my sins, thanking Him for His blessings, and seeking His grace. I want especially to besiege heaven with the prayer that God will do a mighty work in these days, elevating the gospel, reviving His church, and sweeping souls into His kingdom.

As I pray, I always want to remember that what I'm doing is a blood-bought privilege. I wouldn't have access to God at all if it weren't for the fact that Jesus shed His blood on the cross to purchase that access for me.

At this stage of life, I also want to be *more heedful*. I'm talking about paying closer attention to the commandments of the Lord. I want to be more holy. No matter how much holiness a Christian might attain in this life, there's always more to attain. Paul was undoubtedly a holy man, but he confessed that he needed to go further, saying: "Brethren, I do not count myself to have apprehended; but. . . I press toward the goal. . ." (Phil. 3.13a, 14a).

We sorely need to return to stressing holiness in living. Christians are often told these days that someone who says we should keep the Ten Commandments is being legalistic. But it's not legalism to keep what God has commanded. Legalism is requiring God's people to keep something that God hasn't commanded.

The lack of emphasis on holiness in our churches has led to Christians being more and more like the world and it has lessened our influence on the world. Our modern society is having much more success influencing us than we are influencing it.

As I set myself to be more holy in the future, I realize that I've never regretted those times in which I've kept the Lord's commandments. I've always regretted those times in which I didn't.

Finally, I want to be *more hopeful*. There is no uncertainty in the Christian's hope. It isn't a matter of the Christian being unsure about the future and crossing his fingers while he longs for the best. Hope is confident and joyful expectation. It is the Christian knowing what the future holds for him, and rising on his tiptoes with eager expectation to see it. It's the Christian looking forward to meeting Jesus in the air (1 Thess. 4:17) and to inhabiting a new earth in a new body.

Christians are always at their very best when they are most heavenly minded. I want to be more heavenly minded the nearer I get to heaven.

Now you have my "ful"s. There could be more, but I certainly don't want there to be less than thankful, prayerful, heedful, and hopeful. Many of these are expressed in this hymn by Philip Bliss:

More holiness give me, more striving within;
More patience in suff'ring; more sorrow for sin;
More faith in my Savior, more sense of His care;
More joy in His service, more purpose in prayer.

More gratitude give me, more trust in the Lord;
More pride in His glory, more hope in His word;
More tears for His sorrows, more pain at His grief;
More meekness in trial, more praise for relief.

More purity give me, more strength to o'ercome;
More freedom from earth-stains, more longings for home;
More fit for the kingdom, more used would I be;
More blessed and holy, more, Savior, like Thee.

November 29

Are You a Theophilus?

From God's Word, the Bible...

Inasmuch as many have taken in hand to set in order a narrative of those things which have been fulfilled among us, just as those who from the beginning were eyewitnesses and ministers of the word delivered them to us, it seemed good to me also, having had perfect understanding of all things from the very first, to write to you an orderly account, most excellent Theophilus, that you may know the certainty of those things in which you were instructed.

Luke 1:1-4

Luke, whom Paul calls "the beloved physician" (Col. 4:14), wrote two of the books of the New Testament. One is the Gospel that bears his name. The other is the book of Acts. Each of these books was addressed to a man named Theophilus (Luke 1:3; Acts 1:1).

Some think that Luke didn't have a specific individual in mind when he wrote his books. They suggest that he simply used the name Theophilus for any and all of his readers who loved God. But two details that Luke mentions about Theophilus suggest that he, Luke, actually addressed his books to a man by that name.

One of those details is Luke's use of the phrase "most excellent" to describe Theophilus (Luke 1:3). That indicates that Theophilus was a cultured man of high social standing. That makes it very unlikely that Luke was using the name Theophilus as a generic name for all of his readers, as many of them wouldn't have fallen into the category of highly cultured.

Another detail about Theophilus is that he had been instructed in the Christian faith (v. 3) but was evidently experiencing some uncertainty about it. This also indicates that he was a real person. Many of Luke's readers would not have been experiencing the uncertainty that Theophilus was feeling.

But while I assume that Theophilus was an actual individual, he does, in fact, represent those who lack certainty about Christianity. I recently read an article which indicated that most of those who have turned away from the Christian faith say it's because they no longer believe it to be true. The article gave these reasons from three young people who abandoned Christianity:

- "Learning about evolution when I went away to college";
- "Rational thought makes religion go out the window";
- "I just realized somewhere along the line that I didn't really believe it."

It's especially interesting that one student cited evolution as his reason for rejecting Christianity in light of the fact that the more we learn about DNA, the less tenable evolution seems.

And what shall we say to the student who thinks that "rational thought" makes Christianity impossible? We might ask if he or she considers it to be a rational thing to believe something for which there is abundant evidence.

Some people have the notion that there is no evidence for Christianity at all, and that believing it requires laying aside reason to make a blind leap into the dark without any basis for doing so.

There are lots of Theophiluses around. They have had some instruction in Christianity, but they are uncertain about it. Some, like the students mentioned above, have completely abandoned the Christian faith. Others still hold to it, but they do so without any depth of conviction. Like Theophilus of old, they lack certainty about the very thing that they profess to believe.

We don't know how Theophilus came to get in contact with Luke, but it was good for him that he did. Luke was able to assure him that there is "certainty" (v. 4) about "those things which are most surely believed among us" (v. 1).

Luke was talking about the Lord Jesus Christ, as his Gospel and the book of Acts go on to make clear. Christianity is Christ. Take Christ away, and there is no Christianity. Why should we believe in the Lord Jesus Christ? We have substantial evidence for Him. Luke mentions "eyewitnesses" (v. 2). He also claims that he himself had "perfect understanding" of those things that the eyewitnesses reported. With that phrase "perfect understanding," Luke is telling us that he had thoroughly researched the things that were asserted about Christ and had come to the conclusion that they were valid and true. As a result of his research, he was now ready to write his own account of the life and ministry of Jesus.

The Bible plainly declares that there's no need for us to be uncertain about Jesus. It urges us to take a long, hard look at the evidence, and bow before Him as our Savior and Lord. It's always sad when someone chooses to be an unbeliever, but the saddest of all unbelievers is the one who refuses to even look at the evidence for Christ. More about that in the next reading!

November 30

What Is the Evidence for Jesus?

From God's Word, the Bible...

The former account I made, O Theophilus, of all that Jesus began both to do and teach, until the day in which He was taken up, after He through the Holy Spirit had given commandments to the apostles whom He had chosen, to whom He also presented Himself alive after His suffering by many infallible proofs, being seen by them during forty days and speaking of the things pertaining to the kingdom of God.

Acts 1:1-3

What does the Bible affirm about Jesus? It maintains that He was the God-man, that is, God in human flesh and that He came to this earth in order to provide salvation for sinners. Jesus Himself put it in these words: ". . .the Son of Man has come to seek and to save that which was lost" (Luke 19:10).

Are these claims true? Was Jesus really the God-man? Did He actually provide salvation for sinners? In our previous reading we met Theophilus, who was uncertain about these things even though he had received instruction concerning them.

In the opening verses of his Gospel, Luke addressed Theophilus and assured him that he could be certain about the Lord Jesus. The Christian faith is not a leap in the dark. It's not a matter of the Christian crossing his fingers and hoping his beliefs prove to be true.

In his Gospel, Luke laid out things that Jesus said and did (v. 1). His words alone constitute substantial evidence that He was, in fact, God in human flesh. In Luke 4:22, we read: "So all bore witness to Him and marveled at the gracious words which proceeded out of His mouth."

Then there were Jesus' deeds. Luke tells us that Jesus healed the sick (4.38-40; 5:12-15,17-26; 6:6-11,17-19; 7:1-10; 8:43-48, etc.), cast out demons (4:41; 8:26-39), raised the dead (7:11-17; 8:49-56), stilled a storm (8:22-25), and fed a multitude (9:10-17).

In addition to these things, three of His disciples saw Him in His heavenly glory on the Mount of Transfiguration (9:28-36).

Luke closes his Gospel by affirming that Jesus Himself arose from the grave (24:1-43) and ascended to the Father in heaven (24:50-53).

We should keep in mind as we read Luke's accounts of the miracles of Jesus that they were performed before the "eyewitnesses" that he mentions in the opening words of his Gospel (Luke 1:2).

When Luke took up his pen to write the book of Acts, it was so he could continue the story of Jesus. Some people seem to have the idea that Acts is all about the Holy Spirit, but, no, it is about the Lord Jesus. The Holy Spirit was the gift of Christ to His church, and the Holy Spirit's mission in this world is to exalt and glorify Christ.

Luke begins the book of Acts in the same way that he ended his gospel, that is, with the resurrection and ascension of Jesus.

Luke, along with all the early Christians, regarded the resurrection of Jesus as the supreme proof of His claims. No one can read the book of Acts without being impressed with how much emphasis the early disciples gave to the resurrection of Jesus. Luke tells us that Jesus "presented Himself alive after His suffering by many infallible proofs" (v. 3).

Many infallible proofs! Not one or two, but many! And not fabricated things, but proofs! And proofs that are not questionable or debatable but are infallible, that is, unmistakable or unassailable.

In his Gospel, Luke gives some of these many infallible proofs: the large stone covering the tomb of Jesus was rolled away, the body of Jesus was not in the tomb, angels were present to proclaim the resurrection, the cloths in which the body of Jesus had been wrapped were convincingly arranged, and the risen Christ appeared to many (Luke 24:1-43).

The appearances of the risen Christ had to be especially convincing in light of the fact that they were not limited to a single day or two, but were rather stretched out for a period of forty days.

Still another proof of Jesus' resurrection is the tremendous change that His disciples experienced. They went from being resurrection skeptics to being bold advocates of it. And, as the book of Acts so wonderfully details, the truth of Jesus' resurrection took Christianity from a tiny beginning to worldwide influence

We can also add to Jesus' resurrection the truth of His ascension (vv. 9-11), which was also witnessed by many.

The words, deeds, resurrection of Jesus, and ascension of Jesus come together to give us the overwhelmingly powerful testimony that He was indeed God in human flesh, the Savior for sinners, and that He lives today in the glory of heaven.

The question has never been whether there is sufficient evidence for Christianity. It has always been whether we will accept the evidence.

What about you? Are you challenged and encouraged by the words Luke wrote to Theophilus? Are you persuaded, not just intellectually, but in a way that has brought you to warm, personal faith in the Christ who came to bring a full and free salvation to all who turn from sin and trust in Him alone?

"'Till We Meet Again"

A Reading from Sylvia

From God's Word, the Bible...

"Father, I desire that they also whom You gave Me may be with Me where I am, that they may behold My glory which You have given Me; for You loved Me before the foundation of the world."

John 17:24

I was recently blessed to be part of a special reunion. For the last three years my four brothers and I, along with spouses, have been gathering once a year to spend two or three days together. We live in three different states, so time spent with all five of us together rarely happens. Since we are in our 60s and 70s, we realize that we need to be intentional about getting together. Life is speeding by, and we know the time will come when, one by one, we will be departing this life.

This year our sibling reunion was a little different. We invited another group of three siblings, whom we have known since childhood, to join us. These two brothers and a sister attended the same small country church as our family, and our parents were best friends. Growing up, we spent a lot of time together. It was so good to reminisce about our escapades as children and teenagers. One great blessing was sharing memories of our godly parents and the great impact they had on our lives.

It was mentioned more than once during the weekend that we may never all be together again. I was reminded of a scene from my childhood related to that small country church we all attended.

Our church had experienced an unusual revival meeting, the kind today's younger generation of churchgoers know little or nothing about. I'm sure it was at least a two-week meeting, as all of them were in the 1950s. Some meetings even extended into the third week.

In this particular revival, we had experienced an unusual working of the Spirit of God in our midst. Unbelievers had become believers. Wayward believers had been revived. Church members who were at odds with one another had been reconciled. The presence of the Holy Spirit was evident in the worship services each night. As church members went about their day's work, their thoughts were on the joys of the previous evening's service and the anticipation of the coming evening's service. Even as a child, I experienced this blessed phenomenon.

The guest preacher for this revival meeting preached with an unusual anointing of God. In addition to this, he had a warm, winsome spirit about him. Our hearts were knit to him for the person he was, and for the work that God was doing through him.

On the last Sunday of the meeting, the church had planned a potluck farewell dinner for the guest preacher. After the morning preaching service, as we always called it, we went a short distance down the road to the two-room country schoolhouse for the dinner. We had the meal there because at that time our church had no fellowship hall or room large enough to have a meal together.

After the meal was over, the time came for our guest preacher to leave us and return to his home. He lived a long distance from our church, so we were keenly aware that we might never see him again in this life. And, oh, how we had come to love him! He had been God's instrument to bring great blessing to our church. Before he left, we formed a circle around the perimeter of that large room. We held hands and sang the words of Jeremiah Eames Rankin:

God be with you 'till we meet again;
By His counsels guide, uphold you;
With His sheep securely fold you.
God be with you 'till we meet again.
'Till we meet, 'till we meet,
'Till we meet at Jesus' feet;
'Till we meet, 'till we meet,
God be with you till we meet again.

Those of us who attended my family's special reunion may meet again in this life, but that is far from certain. I hope, if we never get together again on this earth, we will meet again at Jesus' feet in heaven's glory where our dear parents are already in the presence of the Lord. Nothing in this world is more important than making sure we are at the feet of Jesus in the eternal world. We can only be sure of that if we bow before Him in this life in true repentance and faith, taking what He did on the cross for sinners as our own. Let each of us heed these words from the Apostle Peter: "Therefore, brethren, be even more diligent to make your calling and election sure. . ." (2 Peter 1:10).

THE MONTH OF DECEMBER

Golden Key and Silver Chain

... And 30 Other Bible-Based Meditations

Jesus identifies Himself as the key to the Bible. I think of Him as the golden key because we associate gold with enormous value, and there's nothing more valuable than the Bible's presentation of Jesus. There is no greater knowledge to be had than the knowledge of Christ. There are no greater riches to be possessed than the riches of Christ. The Bible will be to us as a heavy steel door if we don't insert into its lock the golden key.

Contents

December 1

Golden Key and Silver Chain

From God's Word, the Bible...

"You search the Scriptures, for in them you think you have eternal life; and these are they which testify of Me."

John 5:39

There's a golden key that unlocks the Bible. That key is Jesus. He tells us so. On the day of His resurrection, He met two travelers on the road to Emmaus and "expounded to them in all the Scriptures the things concerning Himself" (Luke 24:27).

There you have it! Jesus believed that all the Old Testament Scriptures concerned Him. Later that day, He met His disciples in Jerusalem and assured them "that all things must be fulfilled which were written in the Law of Moses and the Prophets and the Psalms concerning Me" (Luke 24:44).

To say the Old Testament is not about Jesus is to quarrel with Jesus. That's an unwinnable quarrel.

So Jesus identifies Himself as the key to the Bible. He is its grand subject. In the Old Testament, He is promised. In the New Testament, He is presented.

I am calling this the golden key because we associate gold with enormous value, and there's nothing more valuable than the Bible's presentation of Jesus. There is no greater knowledge to be had than the knowledge of Christ. There are no greater riches to be possessed than the riches of Christ.

The Bible will be to us as a heavy, steel door if we don't insert into its lock the golden key.

It is fascinating to read the Old Testament with the Lord Jesus in mind. Its main characters picture Him, as do its main events. In addition to those characters and events, the Old Testament also offers many explicit promises about Him and His redeeming work. We might say that the Old Testament gives us a chain of people, events, and promises on which the golden key hangs—let's call it a silver chain. A golden key on a silver chain—that's double value! There is inestimable value in Christ, and there is incalculable value in the people, events, and promises that point to Him.

The devotions that follow will deal with some of these people, events, and promises. We will look at ten crucial people, ten crucial pictures (events), and ten crucial promises (prophecies).

These devotions have both believers and unbelievers in mind. My hope for those who believe in Christ is that they will be thrilled and moved to greater worship of Christ and service to Him.

I've been concerned for several years now about believers in Christ falling into the clutches of dull familiarity. That can easily happen. Many of us have been familiar with the glorious truth of Christ for a long time. What a blessing! But our blessing becomes a problem if we let our familiarity with Christ dull our appreciation of Him. Familiarity with glorious truth can put us in the camp of the Ephesian Christians who "left" their first love (Rev. 2:4).

Getting a fresh sight of Christ will go a long way toward helping us love Him as we should, and examining the various links of the silver chain in the Old Testament is one way to get a fresh sight of Him. So, I invite my fellow-believers to join me in looking for the Lord Jesus in various Old Testament people, types, and promises. As we do, let's make this our prayer:

Let me love Thee more and more,
Till this fleeting, fleeting life is o'er;
Till my soul is lost in love,
In a brighter, brighter world above.
(Fanny J. Crosby)

I also hope that people who have not yet come to faith in Christ who pick up this book will read enough to be amazed to learn how consistently and completely Jesus is presented in the Old Testament.

Many unbelievers reject Christ because they assume there is insufficient evidence for Him. They enjoy projecting themselves as being so intelligent that they can't be duped by believing in One for whom there is little or no evidence. And they assume that those who do believe in Him are in the clutches of ignorance and superstition. They would be shocked to know that many Christians—who once assumed that there is no evidence for Christ—began to study the evidence and took Him as their Savior.

The truth about the skeptics is this: they reject Christianity, not because of a lack of evidence, but rather because they don't want to go where the evidence leads.

My invitation to believers and unbelievers is the same: come with me, look for Jesus, and be amazed.

Adam, the Representative Head

From God's Word, the Bible...

"For God knows that in the day you eat of it your eyes will be opened, and you will be like God, knowing good and evil."

Genesis 3:5

We now begin to consider ten people of the Old Testament who picture the Lord Jesus. The first of these is Adam. The human story is the story of two heads. There have only been two. There will never be another. The first head represented the whole human race. That was Adam. The second head represents a new race.

Our first head plunged us all into sin and ruin. Yes, what Adam did counted for us all. God made Adam in His own image and placed him in the garden of Eden with only one commandment. He was not to eat of the tree of knowledge of good and evil.

Adam failed to keep that commandment. He and Eve yielded to the devil's temptation and ate the forbidden fruit.

That act of disobedience counted for us all. Adam's sin was my sin. Adam's sin was your sin. Since his sin was ours, the penalty for it was also ours. What was the penalty for Adam's sin? Death! Not just physical death, but also spiritual and eternal death! Adam didn't die physically on the same day that he disobeyed God, but he did die. He died spiritually that day. He was alienated from God. His mind, which was made to understand the truth of God, was now darkened. His affections, which were made to love God, were now degraded. His will, which enabled him to seek after God, was now deadened.

And the spiritual death that he died that day would bring in its wake both physical and eternal death. The greatest calamity that has ever occurred in all of human history is the first calamity—the one that occurred when Adam disobeyed God.

Many object to this matter of Adam being our representative head. They insist that it wasn't right or fair for God to let Adam represent all of us, as if God doesn't have the right to do with His creatures as He wills!

But the Bible is so plain on Adam's representation that to deny it is to announce that we don't really believe the Bible or accept it as our authority. The Apostle Paul states it very clearly in these words: ". . .through one man sin entered the world and death through sin. . ." (Rom. 5:12). He also says ". . . by the one man's offense many died" (Rom. 5:15).

Paul made similar statements in Romans 5:17, 18 and 19 and also in 1 Corinthians 15:22. Please note in Romans 5 the steady drumbeat of the phrase "one man." That one man was Adam. There can be no doubt about that.

Those who object to the teaching of Adam's headship should ponder why it is that we all sin and we all die. Those who want to disprove Adam's headship can do so if they stop sinning and stop dying. The fact that they can't do so should make them more receptive to what the Bible says about Adam.

God could have left us all under Adam as our head. He was under no obligation to lift us from the sin and death that Adam brought upon us. But God's grace caused Him to pity us and to provide a way of escape from our sin and death.

What did God do? He appointed another representative head—His Son, the Lord Jesus Christ. Jesus came to this earth to succeed where the first Adam failed. He came to be the second and last Adam. To fill this role, Jesus had to take our humanity. He did that when He was born to Mary in Bethlehem. But in taking our humanity, He didn't divest Himself of His deity.

Was the first Adam tempted to sin? So was Jesus (Matt. 4:1-11). But He didn't yield to temptation.

If Adam as our representative head had obeyed God and refused to yield to temptation, he would have secured for all of us right standing with God. He failed. But Jesus, by His perfect obedience, secured for all who believe in Him the righteousness that God demands.

After living that perfect life, Jesus, the second Adam, went to the cross to die a special death. He received on that cross the penalty for sinners. In addition to depriving us of the righteousness we need, Adam's sin had brought upon us the penalty that must be paid before we can ever be accepted by God. That penalty is death in all its forms. Jesus endured that death on the cross.

So Jesus by His life provided the righteousness we need, and by His death paid the penalty.

Adam's failure as the first head cried out for the head of a redeemed race. In Jesus we have that head.

December 3

Abraham, the Promise-Receiver

From God's Word, the Bible...

"I will make you a great nation;
I will bless you
And make your name great;
And you shall be a blessing.
I will bless those who bless you,
And I will curse him who curses you;
And in you all the families of the earth shall be blessed."

Genesis 12:2-3

There are three monumental men in the Old Testament, men who tower over all the others. They are Abraham, Moses, and David. Each of these three men points us toward the Lord Jesus Christ in various ways, as do many of the lesser Old Testament figures.

There are some obvious parallels between Abraham and Christ. As Abraham was chosen and called by God to fill an important role, so was Jesus. As Abraham sojourned as a stranger in the land God promised to give him, so Jesus sojourned as a stranger on this earth.

But I suggest that the main way in which Abraham points to Christ is in the promises that he, Abraham, received from God. When the Lord called Abraham to a new land, He fortified him with seven promises. Abraham would: (1) be made into a great nation (2) be blessed (3) have a great name (4) be a blessing (5) bring blessing to those who blessed him (6) bring cursing to those who cursed him, and (7) bring blessing to all the families of the earth.

Where does the Lord Jesus fit into this? The Apostle Paul emphatically says that the very promises made to Abraham were made to Abraham's Seed, and he identifies that Seed as Christ. Paul writes: "Now to Abraham and his Seed were the promises made. He does not say, 'And to seeds,' as of many, but as of one, 'And to your Seed,' which is Christ" (Gal. 3:16). If the promises made to Abraham were also made to Christ, then Christ would:

- Be made into a great nation. That nation would consist of all those who belong to Him by faith in His redeeming work.
- Be blessed by the Father as He, Jesus, performed the work of redemption.
- Have a great name. Paul writes about this very matter, saying of Jesus: "Therefore God also has highly exalted Him and given Him the name which is above every name, that at the name of Jesus every knee should bow, of those in heaven, and of those on earth, and of those under the

earth, and that every tongue should confess that Jesus Christ is Lord to the glory of God the Father" (Phil. 2:9-11).

- Be a blessing. It's true that Jesus has brought innumerable blessings on people in general and on His people in particular, but this promise may relate even more to people associating the name of Jesus with being blessed, saying something along these lines: "The truly happy and blessed people are those who know Jesus."
- Bless those who bless Him and curse those who curse Him. All individuals in this world are in one of two camps. They either bless Christ or curse Him, that is, they either accept Him or reject Him. Those who accept Him are blessed "with every spiritual blessing" (Eph. 1:3). Those who reject Him will eventually hear Him say: "Depart from Me, you cursed. . ." (Matt. 25:41).
- Bring blessing to all the families of the earth. Matthew Henry calls this "the promise that crowned all the rest." It's the Father's promise to Christ that the good news of His work would be widely disseminated. It tells us that while Abraham was to be the father of a nation, the knowledge of the Messiah wouldn't be limited to that nation. It's true, of course, that Jesus was born into the nation of Israel. But while He came *to* one nation, He didn't come *for* one nation.

Paul captures this promise in these words: "And the Scripture, foreseeing that God would justify the nations by faith, preached the gospel to Abraham beforehand, saying, 'In you all the nations shall be blessed.' So then those who are of faith are blessed with believing Abraham" (Gal. 3:8-9).

This doesn't mean that every single individual will be saved. It rather means the nations will hear the gospel, and the inhabitants of those nations who believe in it will be saved.

Those who are saved by the redeeming work of Christ will finally see the fulfillment of this promise. The redeemed multitude around the throne of God will sing to the Lord Jesus Christ:

. . . You were slain,
And have redeemed us to God by Your blood
Out of every tribe and tongue and people and nation.
(Rev. 5:9)

As we see Christ in the promises God gave to Abraham, we can already see much of their fulfillment. As we see that fulfillment, our faith in Christ should be deepened and our anticipation of the future heightened.

December 4

Melchizedek, the King-Priest

From God's Word, the Bible...

Then Melchizedek king of Salem brought out bread and wine;
he was the priest of God Most High. And he blessed him and said:
"Blessed be Abram of God Most High,
Possessor of heaven and earth;
And blessed be God Most High,
Who has delivered your enemies into your hand."
And he gave him a tithe of all.

Genesis 14:18-20

The book of Genesis introduces us to Melchizedek, who was both a king and a priest. His name means "king of righteousness." Since he ruled over Salem (later to be called Jerusalem), he could also be called "king of peace" (Salem means peace).

While we know little about him, the author of Hebrews holds him up as a type of Christ (Heb. 6:19-7:1). Before we get into that, let's delve into a bit of history. This history has to do with Abraham rescuing his nephew Lot. As you probably know, Lot had moved to the city of Sodom (Gen. 13:1-13). Sodom was, at this time, one of five cities controlled by a king with the cumbersome name Chedorlaomer. Along with three other kings, for twelve years Chedorlaomer had demanded tribute from Sodom and other cities. Having gotten their fill of paying this tribute, the rulers of these cities finally rebelled against Chedorlaomer and his coalition.

That didn't sit well with Chedorlaomer and his associates. They marched against the five rebellious cities. When they came to Sodom, they looted it and took many of its citizens captive, including Lot.

Lot's capture caused Abraham to spring into action. Forming a coalition of his own, he pursued the army of Chedorlaomer, defeated it, and freed Lot and the other captives (vv.13-16).

The king of Sodom was so grateful for Abraham's intervention that he offered to Abraham all the goods that had been recovered.

Now we get to Melchizedek! Abraham refused the goods and chose, instead, to give a tithe to the priest Melchizedek (vv.18-24). So we're finally ready to ask this question: In what ways can he be said to represent Christ?

- While the Bible refers to Melchizedek as "king of righteousness" (Heb.7:2), he could only be an imperfect representation of it. In all of human history, there has only been one person who was perfectly righteous, and that was the Lord Jesus. God demands that same perfect righteousness of us, and we can't meet it. But God accepts the righteousness of Christ on our behalf when we receive the Lord Jesus by faith.

Jesus' death was also connected with righteousness as He received on the cross the righteous penalty that God had pronounced against sinners.

Christianity described in a few words is this: Jesus provided the righteousness we don't have and paid for the sins we do have. What He did applies only to those who trust in Him.

- While the Bible refers to Melchizedek as "king of peace" (Heb. 7:2), the very fact that Abraham was returning from a battle shows that Melchizedek couldn't produce perfect peace in his world. Jesus is the greater "king of peace" who will eventually create a world in which there will be no conflict.
- The fact that no genealogy is given for Melchizedek leaves the impression that he had no parents and that his life was endless (Heb. 7:3). While Melchizedek could only suggest or represent endlessness, the Lord Jesus actually possesses it. His priesthood, in which He represents sinners before God, will continue forever.
- Melchizedek pronounced a blessing upon Abraham (vv.19-20), and the Lord Jesus Christ, as the priest of His people, pronounces blessing upon them as well. All spiritual blessings flow to us, not because of anything we do to earn or deserve them, but solely because of the priestly work of Christ on our behalf.

Abraham responded to Melchizedek's blessing by giving him a tithe (Gen. 14:20). It seems to be very likely that Abraham saw Melchizedek to be a type of the coming Messiah, and that he, Abraham, responded in an appropriate fashion.

The king of Sodom had come to Abraham to offer him the spoils of the battle. Melchizedek came to Abraham to offer a blessing. Abraham refused the first offer and accepted the second.

We should see in Abraham's choice the option set before us. On one hand, we have the righteousness and peace pictured by Melchizedek and truly provided by Christ. On the other hand, we have Satan offering peace and joy that he can't actually produce. God calls us to accept Christ and reject Satan.

December 5

Job, the Righteous Sufferer

From God's Word, the Bible...

Then the Lord said to Satan, "Have you considered My servant Job, that there is none like him on the earth, a blameless and upright man, one who fears God and shuns evil?"

Job 1:8

Job, who probably lived during the time of Abraham, was a righteous man who suffered horrible things. He is described for us as one who was "blameless and upright" and as one who "feared God and shunned evil" (1:1, 9).

But Job's righteousness didn't immunize him from suffering. In quick succession he lost his children, his servants, his possessions, and his health.

These calamities weren't the result of bad luck. Satan had come before God to allege that Job loved God and served Him because God had blessed him. Furthermore, Satan argued that if God were to withdraw those blessings, Job would turn against Him.

The book of Job challenges us to ask ourselves if we love and serve God for His own sake or just to get good things from Him. It compels us to ask ourselves if God is to us a means to get ends that we want or if He is the end that we want.

So God allowed Satan to test Job at this very point: would he continue to be upright even in the loss of children, servants, possessions, and health?

Job, of course, was unaware of what had gone on in heaven between God and Satan. One of the greatest values of the book of Job is its reminder that there is always more going on in our lives than we realize. The book doesn't urge us to abandon our reason. It does tell us that there are many things above our reason.

Job had faith in the coming Christ. That's clear from his tremendous statement of faith:

For I know that my Redeemer lives,
And He shall stand at last on the earth. . . .
(Job 19:25)

But Job also pictures Christ for us in ways that he couldn't have fully understood. As we look at Job's sufferings, we must surely realize that the Lord Jesus was the greater sufferer. Jesus was the more righteous man who suffered greater things with a more willing spirit.

Jesus was more righteous than Job. While the book of Job declares Job to have been righteous, it never says he was perfectly righteous. With all of his goodness, Job was still an imperfect man who committed sins. Jesus is the only person in all of human history who never sinned. He was "without blemish and without spot" (1 Peter 1:19; see also 2 Cor. 5:21 and 1 John 3:5).

And Jesus suffered greater things than Job. We can't minimize the sufferings of Job. They were horrendous. But they could never come near what Jesus suffered. When Jesus' suffering is mentioned, we are often inclined to think of such things as the hostility of those who hated Him, the cruel mockery, the scourging, the crown of thorns, and the physical agonies of crucifixion. These were all very real and painful, but the worst of Jesus' suffering lay in Him becoming sin for us and bearing the wrath that our sins deserve. The worst of His suffering was in those awful hours from noon to three in which He was forsaken of God (Matt. 27:46) so those who believe in Him never have to experience that same forsakenness.

We can be sure that in this life we will never be able to plumb the depths of suffering to which Jesus descended on our behalf. Those depths will finally be revealed to us in eternity, and we will be amazed.

One of the things that should amaze us even now is that Jesus suffered willingly. Job wasn't exactly a willing sufferer. He complained to his three friends, Eliphaz, Bildad, and Zophar, that God wasn't treating Him fairly. When God finally speaks to Job at the end of the book, Job has to "repent in dust and ashes" (42:6).

Jesus, on the other hand, never complained about the suffering that was involved in His mission of redemption. He gladly shouldered the load on our behalf. In Hebrews 12:2, we read that "for the joy that was set before Him," He "endured the cross" and despised "the shame."

There was joy in that cross for Jesus. It was the joy of redeeming sinners. And He kept that joy in view as He suffered the horrors of Calvary.

There's much about Job's suffering that is beyond our ability to understand, but we can understand that it points us to the suffering of Jesus on behalf of sinners. While it's not usually right to rejoice over the suffering of others, we can and should rejoice in the suffering of Jesus because He willingly and lovingly laid down His life for sinners such as we are.

December 6

Joseph, the Savior

From God's Word, the Bible...

The famine was over all the face of the earth, and Joseph opened all the storehouses and sold to the Egyptians. And the famine became severe in the land of Egypt.

Genesis 41:56

Joseph, the great-grandson of Abraham, points us to the Lord Jesus in some marvelous ways. He was greatly loved by his father, hated by his brothers, conspired against, sold, and tempted. But he remained faithful through it all. Each of these details finds a parallel in Christ. And there are also several more interesting parallels.

This reading focuses on the picture of Jesus that Joseph—as the savior of his people—provides for us.

After being sold into slavery in Egypt by his spiteful brothers, Joseph, through a series of almost incredible events, came to prominence there. We remember that he had predicted to Pharaoh that there would be seven years of tremendous abundance followed by seven years of harsh famine.

The years of plenty came, and Joseph used that time to store grain. He "gathered very much grain, as the sand of the sea, until he stopped counting, for it was without number" (v. 49).

When the famine came, the people soon ran out of grain and came to Pharaoh for relief. Pharaoh responded to them by saying: "Go to Joseph; whatever he says to you, do" (v. 55).

The famine was also "over all the face of the earth," so people from other lands began coming to Joseph who "opened all the storehouses" of Egypt (v. 56).

So, Joseph functioned as a savior. He saved people from starvation in a famine-ravaged time. In so doing, he serves as a type of another and far greater Savior, the Lord Jesus Christ.

When we come to the New Testament, we meet another Joseph—the one who was to be joined in marriage to Mary. This Joseph received a visit from an angel, who announced that Mary was to have a special son. The angel said: "Joseph, son of David, do not be afraid to take to you Mary your wife, for that which is conceived in her is of the Holy Spirit. And she will bring forth a Son, and you shall call His name Jesus, for He will save His people from their sins" (Matt. 1:20-21).

Jesus came to this earth to be a far greater Savior than the first Joseph. In what ways is Jesus a better Savior?

First, Joseph opened a temporal storehouse to meet a temporal need; the Lord Jesus opens the storehouse of salvation to meet a spiritual need.

The people of Joseph's time were perishing physically, and his storehouse saved them. But perishing spiritually and eternally is far worse than perishing physically. It is that condition in which we are separated from God because of our sins, that condition which will ultimately issue into perishing eternally. Jesus has a storehouse full of forgiveness for our sins! He has a storehouse of salvation!

Secondly, Joseph had authority to open the storehouse of Egypt; Jesus opens the storehouse of salvation on the basis of far greater authority.

The authority by which Joseph operated was Pharaoh's. The authority by which Jesus operated was God's, and it is to Jesus alone that God has granted authority to open the storehouse of salvation. No one else can do so. Jesus Himself said: "All authority has been given to Me in heaven and in earth" (Matt. 28:18; see also Acts 4:12).

Thirdly, While Joseph did great things to open the storehouses of Egypt, Jesus did far greater things to open the storehouse of salvation.

Joseph had to plan and to work diligently for a period of seven years to make sure that the storehouses of Egypt were full. He had to exercise constant oversight. What did it take for Jesus to open the storehouse of salvation? He had to take our humanity. He had to also live in perfect obedience to God. He had to go to the cross to receive the penalty of eternal wrath in the place of sinners. He lives today to intercede for all those who come to God through Him (Heb. 7:25).

Finally, while those who came to Joseph had to purchase their grain, those who come to Jesus are given salvation.

Salvation cannot be earned or deserved. It is free. Paul said to the Christians of Ephesus: "For by grace you have been saved through faith, and that not of yourselves; it is the gift of God, not of works, lest anyone should boast" (Eph 2:8-9).

When needy people came to Pharaoh for help, he said: "Go to Joseph" (v. 55). We who know Jesus as Savior do not hesitate to say to needy sinners: "Go to Jesus!"

December 7

Judah, the Surety

From God's Word, the Bible...

For your servant became surety for the lad to my father, saying, "If I do not bring him back to you, then I shall bear the blame before my father forever."

Genesis 44:32

Joseph's cup had been found in Benjamin's sack. It had been placed there as the test Joseph had devised to see if his brothers would be willing to let Benjamin go into slavery in Egypt, as they had done with him.

Judah, the brother who had suggested that Joseph be sold to the Midianite traders (Gen. 37:26-27), now spoke to Joseph on behalf of his brother Benjamin. Judah had promised his father Jacob that he would serve as the surety for Benjamin. Now before Joseph, he acts as that surety.

A surety is one who stands good for another. Joseph's cup had been found in Benjamin's sack. Benjamin was, therefore, the one who was under Joseph's sovereign indictment. He was the one who was sentenced to serve as Joseph's slave, a sentence Joseph emphatically stated in these words: ". . .the man in whose hand the cup was found, he shall be my slave" (v. 17).

But Judah had pledged himself to be the surety for Benjamin. As Benjamin's surety, he, Judah, would become the slave of Joseph instead of Benjamin. Even though the cup had not been found in Judah's sack, he would bear the penalty for it. If the penalty were slavery, a slave he would be!

The plea of Judah was so powerful and moving that Joseph "could not restrain himself" any longer. He had to reveal his identity to his brothers (Gen. 45:1-3).

In standing as the surety for Benjamin, Judah portrays the Lord Jesus. He is the surety for His people (Heb. 7:22).

Benjamin needed a surety. Joseph's cup was found in his sack. There was no way to get around it. And we need a surety as well. We might say God's cup is found in our sacks. In other words, God has the goods on us. He has given us commandments by which to live—the Ten Commandments—and we have all failed to keep them. We are sinners. What is it to be a sinner? It is to refuse to conform to the commandments of God.

Is there any hope for us? The answer for Benjamin came in the form of his brother Judah, and the answer for us lies in the Lord Jesus.

There is no cup to be found in the sack of Jesus' life! He was completely without sin (1 Peter 1:19; 1 John 3:5), and was, therefore, free from the indictment of divine justice. He, Jesus, was free to go even as Judah was (v. 17).

But the heart of Jesus was such that he could not be content to let the sentence of God's judgment fall on those He loved while He Himself walked away. The heart of a surety beat inside Jesus! He submitted Himself to the sentence of divine judgment so His people could walk away from it. On the cross, Jesus took the place of His people. He received the wrath that was due them. He went to hell on that cross so His people will never have to endure hell themselves. He became for us a far greater surety than Judah was for Benjamin because He endured a far greater sentence. The Apostle Peter tells us that Jesus "bore our sins in His own body on the tree" (1 Peter 2:24). That tree, of course, was the cross.

If we would avail ourselves of the work of Christ, we must quit defending ourselves against God, admit that His cup is in the sack of our lives, and believe in the saving work of the Lord Jesus Christ.

When Judah stood as the surety for his younger brother, he didn't know for sure that he would be allowed to receive Benjamin's sentence. He must certainly have hoped that Joseph would be merciful and lift from both him and Benjamin the sentence.

It was different with Jesus. He left the glories of heaven and came to this earth will the full knowledge that He would indeed bear the sentence of His people. Knowing full well that there was no way to avoid the sentence, He moved relentlessly toward it, and, in so doing, took all His people from being slaves of sin to being children of God. So, we now say with the Apostle John: "Behold what manner of love the Father has bestowed on us, that we should be called children of God!" (1 John 3:1).

December 8

Moses, the Mediator

From God's Word, the Bible...

So Moses came and called for the elders of the people, and laid before them all these words which the Lord commanded him. Then all the people answered together and said, "All that the Lord has spoken we will do." So Moses brought back the words of the people to the Lord.

Exodus 19:7-8

In the earlier reading on Abraham, I identified Moses as one of the three monumental men of the Old Testament. God used Moses to deliver the Israelites from bondage in Egypt. He used him to constitute them into a nation; He used him to serve as a prophet to the nation; and He used him to lead the nation.

In these various facets of Moses' life, we get glimpses of the Lord Jesus. Jesus delivers sinners from bondage to sin and Satan; Jesus constitutes His people into a "holy nation" (1 Peter 2:9); and Jesus is the prophet who declares truth to His people. Jesus also leads His people.

There's another role that Moses filled, and in that role he supplies us with the best picture of the Lord Jesus. That role is mediator. A mediator is a go-between. Exodus 19 provides us one example of Moses serving as the mediator between God and the Israelites. God spoke to the people through Moses (v. 7), and the people spoke to God through Moses (v. 8).

Why did God deal with the Israelites in this way? Why didn't He speak directly to the people and allow them to speak directly to Him? By using Moses as His mediator, God was driving home this powerful truth: He is holy, and the only way sinners can approach Him is through the mediator that He has appointed.

One way that God demonstrated His holy character to the Israelites was by having boundaries set around Mt. Sinai so the people couldn't come near it or touch it (vv. 12-13, 23-24).

Some lightly dismiss Exodus 19. As far as they are concerned, God is not the way that He was in Old Testament times. He is now loving and kind instead of serious and severe.

But the Bible affirms that God never changes (Mal. 3:6). We're dealing with the same God today as the Israelites of old. He is as holy today as He was then, and the gap between God in His holiness and sinners in their sins is terrifically wide. Our sins have put us at odds with God and in conflict with Him.

We need a mediator! We need someone to come between us in our sins and God in His holiness. Can such a mediator be found? The glad answer of the Bible is this: "For there is one God and one Mediator between God and men, the Man Christ Jesus. . ." (1 Tim. 2:5).

Jesus is a far better mediator than Moses ever was. Moses was an imperfect mediator because he himself was a sinful man.

Jesus is the perfect mediator. As God Himself, He could perfectly represent God. He came to this earth as a human being, adding to His deity our humanity. Now He could also perfectly represent us. Jesus was the God-man, fully God and fully man at one and the same time.

Jesus came to this earth to satisfy God's holy demands and to enable us to meet those holy demands. God demands that we be perfectly righteous to enter heaven. Jesus met that demand as He lived a perfectly righteous life. God demands that our sins, which disqualify us from heaven, be paid for. Jesus met that demand as He died on the cross.

When God's justice looks upon the perfect life of Christ and upon His sin-bearing death, it has to relinquish its hold on sinners. Christ has fully met its demands. On the basis of what Christ has done, God can and does pronounce guilty sinners as guiltless. Through Christ, we who were in conflict with God are now at peace, saying with Paul: "Therefore, having been justified by faith, we have peace with God through our Lord Jesus Christ" (Rom. 5:1).

Augustus Toplady, having found peace with God through Christ, celebrated that peace with these words:

The terrors of law and of God
With me can have nothing to do;
My Saviour's obedience and blood
Hide all my transgressions from view.

The one who rests on the mediation of the Lord Jesus Christ doesn't have to live in fear and dread of having to meet the holy God. The terrors of the God of Mt. Sinai have yielded to the Christ of Mt. Calvary because Jesus is "the Mediator of the new covenant" (Heb. 12:24).

December 9

Aaron, the Atonement-Maker

From God's Word, the Bible...

Then Aaron took it as Moses commanded, and ran into the midst of the assembly; and already the plague had begun among the people. So he put in the incense and made atonement for the people.

Numbers 16:47

Numbers 16 is the ghastly chapter with the glorious end. The ghastly part is the rebellion with which this chapter begins. This rebellion, led by Korah, Dathan, Abiram, and others (v. 1) was directed against Moses and Aaron, the God-ordained leaders of Israel.

It didn't last long. God put an end to it by opening the earth to swallow the rebels (vv. 31-33).

That would seem to have put an end to all opposition to Moses and Aaron, but, shockingly enough, it didn't. The very next day "all the congregation of the children of Israel murmured against Moses and Aaron" (v. 41). This shows us how deeply entrenched sin is in human nature.

Now we come to this chapter's glorious end. God had already begun to visit this further expression of rebellion with some sort of plague. Quickly discerning what was happening, Moses told Aaron to take fire from the altar, put incense on it, and "make atonement" for the people (v. 46).

The action that Aaron took provided atonement. It satisfied the wrath of God against the sin of the people. It took their sin out of the way so that they could be at one with God or at peace with God.

How did Aaron's action accomplish this? We must keep in mind that we have here the high priest of Israel coming between God and the people and offering incense to God. This satisfied God. We know Aaron's atonement was effective because "the plague stopped" (v. 48).

The glory of this chapter, then, is the glory of atonement. The word "atonement" means "the making of one" or "to make at one with." The people of Israel were not at one with God. Their sin had alienated them from Him. Before they could be at one with God, their sin had to be dealt with or God's wrath against their sin had to be appeased.

This episode provides us with a picture of ourselves. We all need atonement. We come into this world in a state of alienation from God. Although God created us, sin has kept us from being at one with Him. And there's no way we can ever have that oneness until our sins are taken out of the way.

As Aaron made atonement for his people on that occasion, so Jesus has made atonement for His people. He did so by going to the cross. There he stood between the dead—spiritually dead sinners—and the living God. He was on that cross in the capacity of the high priest of His people. He offered himself on their behalf. He received God's wrath that was going out toward His people. In receiving it, He exhausted it. He didn't receive *some* of God's wrath so that His people would only have to bear the rest. He received it *all* so that they would have to bear none.

And as God the Father looked upon that cross and saw the flickering embers of what had been His holy wrath against sin, He was satisfied. That death was like sweet incense to Him. His nostrils had been filled with the stench of our sins and the burning of His own wrath, but the death of Christ was like a soothing aroma to Him. It replaced the stench. He smelled that aroma and was satisfied. This is why the Apostle Paul wrote these words: ". . .Christ also has loved us and given Himself for us, an offering and a sacrifice to God for a sweet-smelling aroma" (Eph. 5:2).

Henry Mahan moves from Aaron to Christ by saying:

> The people were dropping like dust as Aaron stepped between them and God to plead God's mercy for them. He was in effect saying, "Death and judgement, you must march over me and my atonement; you must smite God's high priest and ignore God's atonement if you destroy the people." Wrath and judgement have a claim on us. Justice is ready to smite the sheep. But Christ, the Mediator, stands between us and the justice of God and says, "You must walk over me and ignore my blood to destroy my sheep. . . ."[9]

We should see in Aaron positioning himself between God's wrath and the people a picture of Christ putting Himself in the same position on the cross. And we should be thankful for that picture.

9 Henry Mahan, *With New Testament Eyes*, Evangelical Press, 1993, vol. i, p. 68

December 10

David, the Warrior, King, and Writer

From God's Word, the Bible...

Then Samuel took the horn of oil and anointed him in the midst of his brothers; and the Spirit of the Lord came upon David from that day forward. So Samuel arose and went to Ramah.

1 Samuel 16:13

You see in the title for this reading the three words that come to my mind when I think of David—warrior, king, and writer.

David was a warrior. There can be no doubt about that. He burst on the scene in Israel by defeating Goliath. But that was only the first in a long line of the victories he won for Israel.

David was Israel's great king, ruling over the nation with unusual skill and wisdom. Ask someone who knows his or her Bible to name Israel's greatest king, and he or she will probably mention David.

David was a writer, composing more than 73 of the 150 psalms. I say "more than" because he evidently wrote more psalms than the 73 that bear his name. Psalm 2 doesn't carry David's name, but the early church attributed it to him (Acts 4:25).

In each of his major roles, David serves as a picture of the Lord Jesus Christ. David's greatest victory as a warrior came when he defeated the nine-feet tall Philistine giant, Goliath (1 Sam. 17:1-58).

For many years, now, it has been trendy for Christians to look to this account for tips on how to defeat the "giants" in their lives. We do better if we see in this story a greater David defeating a greater enemy to achieve a greater deliverance. The greater David is the Lord Jesus. The greater enemy is Satan. And the greater deliverance is deliverance from sin and Satan through the salvation provided by Christ. The Apostle Paul affirms that believers have been "delivered. . . from the power of darkness" (Col. 1:13).

By the way, David defeated Goliath with a sling and a stone. What unlikely instruments! The Lord Jesus defeated Satan by an even more unlikely instrument—a Roman cross!

As the king over Israel, David pictured the kingly office of the Lord Jesus Christ. Jesus' kingdom is not of this world. It is now spiritual in nature, as He rules in the hearts of His people (John 18:36-37). A day will come in which the kingdom of Christ will be openly and universally seen (1 Cor. 15:24-28; Rev. 11:15).

We can't think of David's rule over Israel without realizing how imperfect it was. He could have done a better job of managing the moving of the Ark of the Covenant (2 Sam. 6:1-15). He committed adultery with Bathsheba, had her husband killed, and attempted to cover up the whole sordid affair (2 Sam. 11:1-12:23). David mishandled his son Absalom to such a degree that it almost cost him his kingdom (2 Sam. 13:1-19:43). He conducted a census of the people, although God had strictly forbidden it (2 Sam. 24:1-25).

Each of these failings doesn't nullify or void David as a type of Christ. They rather show us that he was an imperfect type of Christ, and they should drive us to an even greater appreciation of Christ, who has been and is the King who never fails.

God Himself used David's kingship to point to the kingship of the Lord Jesus. God said to David: "And your house and your kingdom shall be established forever before you. Your throne shall be established forever" (2 Sam. 7:16).

The word "forever," used twice in that verse, carries us beyond David himself to the eternal realm. No earthly king or kingdom can last forever. But the kingdom of Christ will last forever (Luke 1:30-33).

As a writer, David didn't picture Jesus as a writer because Jesus left us no written works. But in his writing, David points us to Christ in psalms that are either indirectly messianic (18, 20, 21, 45, 69, 72, 89, 101, 132, 144) or explicitly messianic (2, 22, 110, 118).

David is one of the main links in the Old Testament chain that leads to Christ. As we have seen, he either pictures Christ or points to him. David was placed in a very unusual and privileged position. His son was his Lord! The Messiah would be his son in that he would be one of David's descendants. But the Messiah would also be his Lord in that He would be God in human flesh. David looked forward in faith to the coming Christ. What David eagerly anticipated finally came to pass when his descendants, Joseph and Mary, journeyed to his birthplace, the village of Bethlehem. There Jesus was born, David's son and David's Lord.

As King, Jesus is Lord, the mighty One who is able to save completely all who come to Him by faith. Is He your Lord and Savior?

Nehemiah, the Builder

From God's Word, the Bible...

Then I said to them, "You see the distress that we are in, how Jerusalem lies waste, and its gates are burned with fire. Come and let us build the wall of Jerusalem, that we may no longer be a reproach."

So I sent messengers to them, saying, "I am doing a great work, so that I cannot come down. Why should the work cease while I leave it and go down to you?"

Nehemiah 2:17; 6:3

Let's review. Because of their sinfulness, most of the citizens of Jerusalem were carried into captivity in Babylon in 586 BC. After being the dominant world power for quite a time, Babylon had finally been conquered by the Persians. The Persian king, Cyrus, issued a decree that released the Jews from captivity and allowed them to return to Jerusalem.

Most of the Jews took advantage of that decree and made their way home. Some chose to stay in Persia. Nehemiah was one of those. He had a prestigious position there, serving as cupbearer to the king. Nehemiah seems to have been enjoying his life in Persia. But that changed when a delegation arrived from Jerusalem to lay before Nehemiah facts about that city's terrible condition. They described Jerusalem as being in "great distress and reproach," and added: "The wall of Jerusalem is also broken down, and the gates are burned with fire" (1:3).

This report caused Nehemiah great distress. It drove him to prayer and compelled him to ask the king of Persia for a leave of absence (2:1-6).

Upon arriving in Jerusalem, Nehemiah took the lead in rebuilding the wall. The work would be hard and long, and the difficulties and obstacles were probably more challenging and numerous than Nehemiah ever expected. But he and his workers persevered until the work was done.

Nehemiah makes me think of Jesus in a couple of very important ways. One is that he obviously had a heart for the work. He loved Jerusalem and yearned to see her flourish. He hated seeing her in such a low condition. Nehemiah understood how vital it was for Jerusalem to have a wall. For a city to be without a wall was "a reproach" (2:17). It was an embarrassment. It caused those around them to heap insults and scorn on them. It was also dangerous. The city without a wall was easy prey. Nehemiah's love for Jerusalem was such that he considered the building of the wall to be "this good work" (2:18).

Doesn't all of that make you think of Jesus? It should. The Lord Jesus loves His church even more than Nehemiah loved Jerusalem, and He is committed to building her. He said: ". . .on this rock I will build My church, and the gates of Hades shall not prevail against it" (Matt. 16:18).

The Lord Jesus considered the matter of building His church to be such a good work that He left the glories of heaven to come to this earth to build His church.

Building the wall of Jerusalem was a very costly venture for Nehemiah. He had to leave the comfort and security of Persia to face many threats. Building His church required Jesus to leave the glory and comfort of heaven to die a special death on the cross. That death was the means by which Jesus made the church His own and began building her. The Apostle Paul says: "Christ also loved the church and gave Himself for it" (Eph. 5:25).

That brings me to a second way in which Nehemiah makes me think of Jesus. Tobiah and Sanballat, a couple of unsavory fellows, opposed the rebuilding of Jerusalem's wall. They pretended to want to sit down and talk with Nehemiah, but he saw that their real intent was to do him harm (6:2). So Nehemiah refused by saying to them: "I am doing a great work, so that I cannot come down. Why should the work cease while I leave it and go down to you?" (6:3).

Jesus was on the cross to do a great work. He was there to provide salvation for sinners so they could be part of the church He is building. While Jesus was on the cross, the religious leaders of the Jews gathered round Him and said: "If He is the King of Israel, let Him now come down from the cross, and we will believe Him" (Matt. 27:42).

Those cruel mockers didn't realize it, but Jesus did indeed have the power to step down from the cross. But as Nehemiah refused to come down from the wall, Jesus refused to come down from the cross. He stayed there until He cried: "It is finished!" (John 19:30). Because Jesus refused to come down from the cross, we have salvation.

We should be thankful for Nehemiah and the glimpses that he gives us of Jesus, but we should be even more thankful for Jesus Himself. As the Apostle Paul once wrote to the believers in Corinth, referring to God's gift of salvation in Christ, "Thanks be to God for His indescribable gift!" (2 Cor. 9:15).

December 12

Noah's Ark

FROM GOD'S WORD, THE BIBLE...

And God said to Noah, "The end of all flesh has come before Me, for the earth is filled with violence through them; and behold, I will destroy them with the earth."

GENESIS 6:13

Now we turn out attention to ten events of the Old Testament that picture Christ. We begin with Noah and the ark. I can't read the account of Noah in Genesis without thinking of these words from Hebrews 11:7—"By faith, Noah, being divinely warned of things not yet seen, moved with godly fear, prepared an ark for the saving of his household. . . ."

Noah lived thousands of years ago. He didn't drive a car, watch television, surf the Internet or send texts, but *there's a way that we are all exactly like Noah.* Noah was warned by God "of things not yet seen." Noah was told of judgment to come (Gen. 6:11-13). This judgment was to come in the form of a great flood. God warned Noah about this, and Noah warned others.

We have also been warned by God of judgment to come. Where is this warning? It is in the Bible. Even if a person doesn't read or believe the Bible, the warning is there. The Bible tells us that this world is not all that there is. It says: ". . .it is appointed for men to die once, but after this the judgment. . ." (Heb. 9:27, see also Rom. 14:12).

Judgment Day isn't going to be the same for everyone. Some will hear the Lord say: "Come, you blessed of My Father, inherit the kingdom prepared for you from the foundation of the world. . ." (Matt. 25:34). Others will hear these solemn words: "Depart from Me, you cursed, into the everlasting fire prepared for the devil and his angels. . ." (Matt. 25:41).

This isn't popular teaching. People want human justice and are outraged when criminals go unpunished. But they don't want divine justice. They want God to look past their sins as if those sins had never been committed. That amounts to wanting God to deny His own justice. This He will never do. Our only hope lies not in God denying His justice, but rather in His justice being satisfied as it pertains to us.

There's also a way in which we cannot be like Noah. Hebrews 11:7 tells us that Noah "prepared an ark." After God told Noah about the coming flood, He told him to build an ark. That ark would be the means of salvation for Noah and his family. The great storm that was coming would strike the ark, but it wouldn't strike Noah and his family because they would be safe inside the ark.

Is there an ark of safety to protect us from God's eternal wrath? There is! That ark is the Lord Jesus Christ. Noah's ark is a picture or type of Him. But there is a difference. Noah had to build his own ark, but God doesn't tell us to construct our own plan of salvation. Rather, He tells us that He has constructed it for us in His Son. All that remains is for us to get into the ark that God has provided for us—and more about that shortly!

How is it that Jesus is our ark of safety in the face of eternal judgment? When He was on the cross, God's wrath was on Him. Just as the rain fell and fell on Noah's ark but didn't fall on him, so on the cross the wrath of God fell and fell on Jesus. That same wrath will not fall on those who are in Him.

There's also a way in which we should all be like Noah. Looking once again to Hebrews 11:7, we see that Noah did what he did "by faith."

We can't build our own ark of salvation. God has already done that in Christ. But as Noah got into the ark to escape the flood, we can and must get into Christ in order to escape the judgment to come.

How do we get into Christ as our ark of safety? It is by faith. Faith is taking God at His Word. When Noah heard God's message about the flood that was to come and the ark that he was to build, He believed and acted. God has told us about judgment to come and about the ark He has provided for us in Christ. He now calls us to stop believing the foolishness of the world and to trust in Christ as our Lord and Savior.

December 13

Abraham Offering Isaac

FROM GOD'S WORD, THE BIBLE...

Then Abraham lifted his eyes and looked, and there behind him was a ram caught in a thicket by its horns. So Abraham went and took the ram, and offered it up for a burnt offering instead of his son.

GENESIS 22:13

Abraham knew Isaac had to live. Even though God had commanded him to offer Isaac as a sacrifice, Abraham knew Isaac had to live. The reason Abraham knew is because he had a promise from God. The promise was that he, Abraham, would have descendants through Isaac (Gen. 17:15,16). At this point, there were no descendants. If there were to be descendants, Isaac had to live.

So Abraham was caught between seemingly contradictory words. One word called for Isaac to live, the other for him to die. What was Abraham to do? Was he to believe one word and not the other? Was he to believe neither word?

Abraham solved the dilemma by believing both words. If God wanted him to sacrifice Isaac, he would, but he would also keep believing that Isaac would live. The author of Hebrews tells us that Abraham took into account that "God was able to raise him up, even from the dead" (Heb. 11:19).

So it was off to the mountain and up the mountain for Abraham and Isaac (v. 2). We know how the account ends. Abraham didn't have to offer his son. Isaac was on the altar and the knife was in his father's hand when God intervened. Isaac wouldn't have to die because God determined that a substitute would die in his place. Nearby was a ram with its horns caught in a thicket. That ram would be the sacrifice instead of Isaac (v. 13).

Why? Yes, why? Why would God put Abraham through this experience? The answer is that God was taking Abraham to an even higher level of faith in the coming Messiah. God was preaching the gospel to Abraham on the day that he placed Isaac on that altar. God's command to Abraham to offer his son made Isaac a type of Christ. The author of Hebrews affirms that Abraham received his son from the dead "in a figurative sense" (Heb. 11:19).

God spared Abraham's son that day, but there would come a day in which God would not spare His own Son (Rom. 8:32). There was no ram in the thicket to offer when Jesus died. There was no ram with his horns caught in thorns when Jesus was hanging on the cross with the crown of thorns on His head. There was no ram for Jesus because Jesus was the lamb for us.

God went through with the sacrifice of His Son, and how we should rejoice that He did. Had He not done so, there would be no salvation for us. There, on that cross, God provided such a sufficient substitute for sinners that all who will trust in Christ will be forgiven of their sins.

We can be sure that Abraham came down from Mount Moriah that day with a light step and a happy heart. In addition to not having to offer his son, Abraham had received from the Lord a much better understanding of what the Messiah would do in the place of sinners. He must have kept repeating to himself what the Lord had said: "The Lord will provide." And provide God did. He sent His Son to this earth and to the cross, and, in doing so, provided salvation. It's not at all unlikely that Jesus' cross was placed on the very spot where Abraham built the altar of sacrifice for his son.

By the grace of God, Abraham understood that his personal salvation from sin and his entrance into heaven rested entirely on what God would do through the death of His Son. Abraham looked forward in faith to the coming and dying of Jesus, as did all the Old Testament saints, and he was saved. We must never think that God first tried one plan of salvation, then another and another. God has always had only one way of saving sinners. That way is His Son dying on the cross. Abraham saw that, believed it, and was saved. Jesus Himself said to the religious leaders of His day: "Your father Abraham rejoiced to see My day, and he saw it and was glad" (John 8:56).

If Abraham had known these words to be later penned by Ethel Taylor, he might have sung them as he and Isaac came down the mountain:

Calvary covers it all,
My past with its sin and stain;
My guilt and despair
Jesus took on Him there,
And Calvary covers it all.

December 14

Jacob's Ladder

From God's Word, the Bible...

Then he dreamed, and behold, a ladder was set up on the earth, and its top reached to heaven; and there the angels of God were ascending and descending on it.

Genesis 28:12

Jesus never hesitated to relate Old Testament stories to Himself. Jacob's ladder is one instance. When Jesus called Nathanael to be His disciple, He promised him that he would see "heaven open, the angels of God ascending and descending upon the Son of Man" (John 1:51).

Jacob had been a rotten fellow. He was a conniving scoundrel who had deceived his father and cheated his brother. If he didn't leave home, his brother, Esau, would probably kill him. So leave he did. He was headed to his uncle Laban's house in far-away Padan Aram (v. 5).

Before he left home, his father Isaac had pronounced upon him "the blessing of Abraham" (v. 4). As Jacob lay down on this particular night, those words may very well have been ringing in his ears. He was nothing at all like his grandfather Abraham, and here he was leaving the very land that had been promised to Abraham.

It must have seemed to Jacob that he pulled the plug on all of God's promises, and that heaven was forever closed to him. He was in for a surprise. As he slept, he saw a ladder extending all the way from earth to heaven with angels going up and down the ladder. And God Himself was above the ladder to give him a wonderful message of encouragement and comfort (vv. 12-15).

Jacob couldn't have complained if God had given him a very different dream—one in which there was no ladder at all between earth and heaven, one in which the gates of heaven were barred and chained with scowling angels as guards. God doesn't have to open heaven to sinners. He would be justified if He were to leave heaven closed and sinners in their sins. But God is also gracious, and, in grace, He has done everything necessary for us to enter heaven.

It's important to note that God revealed the ladder to heaven while Jacob was sleeping. That made it clear. Jacob could do nothing to earn God's favor. All he could do was receive that which God was revealing.

Jacob's dream speaks powerfully to those who are carrying a tremendous load of guilt, to those who assume that they have done such horrible things that there is now no way for them to ever enter heaven. There is a way to heaven! There is a ladder that reaches all the way from this earth to heaven itself. That way is Jesus. He is that ladder. Jesus Himself said: "I am the way, the truth, and the life. No one comes to the Father except through Me" (John 14:6).

How is Jesus the way to heaven? God demands that we be perfectly righteous and that our sins be removed before we can enter heaven. We don't have the righteousness God requires. But Jesus came to this earth in our humanity to live that life that we have refused to live. By His perfect life, He provided the righteousness that we lack.

What about our sins? There is only one way that they can be removed. The penalty for sin has to be paid. Jesus, who provided the righteousness that we don't have, also paid for the sin that we do have. He did this on the cross. There He received the wrath of God in the place of sinners so all those who repent of their sin and trust in Him don't have to receive that same penalty. Here it is in a nutshell for all who trust Christ—He got our sin, we get His righteousness. Paul tells us that God made Jesus "who knew no sin to be sin for us, that we might become the righteousness of God in Him" (2 Cor. 5:21).

How do we know that Jesus is the way to heaven? As we look at His life, death, resurrection, and ascension into heaven, we can see the angels of God ascending and descending upon Him, just as He promised Nathanael. In other words, as we look at Jesus, we can see the signature of heaven upon Him. It is there in the words that He spoke, in the miracles that He performed, in the prophecies He fulfilled, in the death that He died, and in the grave that He conquered.

Jacob was overwhelmed by his dream (vv. 16-17). We should be overwhelmed that God would open heaven to us through Christ.

December 15

The Burning Bush

FROM GOD'S WORD, THE BIBLE...

And the Angel of the Lord appeared to him in a flame of fire from the midst of a bush. So he looked, and behold, the bush was burning with fire, but the bush was not consumed.

EXODUS 3:2

The incarnation of Christ, the crucifixion of Christ, and the resurrection of Christ all depicted in one desert bush! In a bush? Yes, in a bush! Stay tuned.

Moses was on the back of the desert tending the sheep of his father-in-law. There was such sameness about shepherding that it's safe to say that Moses wasn't expecting anything out of the ordinary on this particular day. But out of the ordinary is exactly what he experienced. A burning bush suddenly caught his eye and drew his attention. The mere fact that the bush was burning wasn't so extraordinary. It was rather the fact that the bush wasn't consumed by the fire. It kept burning and burning without being burned up.

As Moses drew near, the extraordinary bush became even more extraordinary. Moses could both see the Angel of the Lord in that bush and hear Him speak. We have here a miracle within a miracle. The first is the bush burning without being consumed. The second is the Angel of the Lord appearing in the burning bush.

We must not think that the Angel of the Lord was an ordinary angel, as if there is such a thing as an ordinary angel! The Angel of the Lord was actually the Lord Himself.

It's understandable that Moses wanted to get a better view of this bush (v.3). But as he approached, the Lord said: "Do not draw near this place. Take your sandals off your feet, for the place where you stand is holy ground" (v. 5).

The Lord calls us to reverence Him as we recognize His greatness and holiness. How we need to hear that call! In this day of easy, breezy familiarity with God, there seems to be little consciousness of how great God is and how unworthy we are.

The fact that the Lord stooped so very low to appear in a lowly bush pictures for us the incarnation of Christ. What was the distance between the glory of heaven and that desert bush? It must be about the same as the distance between the glory of heaven and our humanity. That is the distance Jesus traversed when He took our humanity.

The fact that the Lord appeared in the bush didn't mean that He ceased to be the Lord. And the fact that Jesus appeared on this earth in our humanity didn't mean that He ceased to be God. In coming to this earth, Jesus didn't subtract His deity. He added our humanity. He was still God even though He was in human flesh. The Apostle John put it in these words: "The Word became flesh and dwelt among us, and we beheld His glory, the glory as of the only begotten of the Father, full of grace and truth" (John 1:14).

The fact that the Lord was not only in the bush but also in "a flame of fire" pictures for us the crucifixion of Jesus. We might say that the Lord was in the bush so He could be in the fire.

Fire represents judgment. To say the Lord came to this earth to go through fire is to say He came here to go through judgment for us. That's exactly what He did on the cross.

Why was it necessary for Jesus to go through judgment for us? It was to keep those who trust in Him from going through that judgment themselves. Our sins deserve God's judgment, and that judgment is most fearful indeed—eternal separation from God. On the cross, Jesus went through the fire of God's judgment. He endured the fire of separation from the Father (Matt. 27:46).

The fact that the bush Moses saw wasn't consumed points us to a most glorious truth indeed—the Lord who was in the fire of God's judgment on the cross wasn't consumed by that fire. The cross wasn't the final word about Jesus. Yes, He died there and was buried, but He arose in complete victory on the third day.

When Moses saw the burning bush in the desert, he said: "I will now turn aside and see this great sight" (v. 3).

The Bible sets Christ before us—incarnate, crucified, and risen—and it urges each of us to turn aside from our sins and trust in His redeeming work.

December 16

The Passover

From God's Word, the Bible...

"Now the blood shall be a sign for you on the houses where you are. And when I see the blood, I will pass over you; and the plague shall not be on you to destroy you when I strike the land of Egypt."

Exodus 12:13

The people of Israel had been slaves in Egypt for more than four hundred years when God moved to deliver them through the leadership of Moses. Pharaoh, the leader of Egypt, viewed the matter quite differently. Israelite slavery was so vital to the Egyptian economy that Pharaoh wasn't about to free the Israelites. He would need persuasion, and that's exactly what God provided for him by sending nine devastating plagues upon Egypt.

Pharaoh, being a stubborn fellow, still refused to release the Israelites. So one more plague was in order—the tenth and last plague. God was going to send His death angel over the land to slay all the firstborn. That sentence of death for the firstborn would have been carried out against the Israelites also if God hadn't made a special provision for them. But a special provision is exactly what God gave His people. If they would slay lambs, mark their doors with the blood of those lambs, and stay inside those blood-marked doors, they would be spared. The death angel would pass over them.

It all went according to God's script. The Israelites killed their lambs, marked their doors, and stayed inside their houses. The angel carried out his mission of death, sparing the Israelites while visiting Pharaoh and all the Egyptians. Having seen enough, Pharaoh decided to let the people of Israel go.

The Passover is a historical event with ongoing significance. It released the Israelites from their bondage in Egypt, but it also pointed those Israelites to an even greater Passover. That Passover would be their long-awaited Messiah, the Lord Jesus Christ. The Apostle Paul made this connection when he called Christ "our Passover" (1 Cor. 5:7).

Christians don't hesitate to call Christ their Passover because they know that through Him they have been saved from a far worse slavery, a far greater Pharaoh, and a far worse sentence than the Israelites of old.

Our greater slavery was the slavery of sin. Our greater Pharaoh was the devil himself. And our far worse sentence wasn't the physical death doled out by the angel in Egypt. It was the eternal death or eternal wrath that we stood to receive before Christ saved us. Paul neatly expresses it all when he says of

Christ: “Much more then, having now been justified by His blood, we shall be saved from wrath through Him” (Rom. 5:9).

Just as putting the blood of those lambs on their doors saved the Israelites, so we are saved from eternal wrath by the blood of Christ.

Why does God insist on the shedding of blood as the way of salvation? It represents the pouring out of life in death. The penalty for sin is death. We can't have forgiveness if that penalty isn't paid. The shedding of blood in death means that the penalty for sin is paid.

When Jesus died on the cross, that is, when He shed His blood there, He was paying the penalty for sins so all who believe in Him will never have to pay that same penalty.

Perhaps someone is wondering how the physical blood of Jesus or His physical death could really pay for sin, which is spiritual in nature. How could Jesus' physical death pay for a spiritual problem? There are depths of meaning in His death that we can never fathom in this life, but we can say this: the physical shedding of Jesus' blood represented something far greater than physical death. His physical death was the outward and visible representation of something far greater than physical death. It represented Him being separated from God (spiritual death) and receiving the wrath of God (eternal death).

How could Jesus experience all that on the cross? We must always keep in mind that Jesus was a special person. He was God in human flesh—the God-man. So He could—and did—experience on the cross things that a mere man couldn't experience.

It's enough for us to know that the shedding of Jesus' blood saves all those who repent of their sins and trust in Him. If we want God to pass over us and not visit us in judgment, we must lay hold of the redeeming work of Christ by faith. It isn't enough to know that Jesus died on the cross; we must personally trust in Him in what He did there. The Israelites were not saved from death merely because they were Israelites. They were saved by blood. If we want God to pass over us on Judgment Day, we must trust in the shed blood of Christ, God's ultimate Passover Lamb.

December 17

The Crossing of the Red Sea

From God's Word, the Bible...

And Moses said to the people, "Do not be afraid. Stand still, and see the salvation of the Lord, which He will accomplish for you today. For the Egyptians whom you see today, you shall see again no more forever. The Lord will fight for you, and you shall hold your peace."

Exodus 14:13-14

What a predicament! The people of Israel had been released from their slavery in Egypt and now had the Red Sea before them, and Pharaoh and his army behind them. There seemed to be no way of escape.

All of the Israelites were "very afraid" (v. 13). Some, in a terrific fit of illogic, concluded that they had been delivered from Egypt so they could die in the wilderness (vv. 11-12).

Moses assured the people that the Lord would fight for them (v. 14), and the Lord did. He commanded Moses to lift his rod over the sea (v. 16), and He promised that the sea would open as the people went forward (v. 15). That's exactly what happened. With a wall of water on each side, and with the ground under their feet being dry, the Israelites were able to get safely across. When the army of Egypt attempted to follow, Moses again stretched his rod over the sea, and those walls of water came crashing down on the Egyptians. To put it in a nutshell, God's people were saved and their enemy was destroyed (vv. 21-30).

The situation at the Red Sea seemed to be so utterly hopeless and impossible. But God made a way.

It makes me think of another seemingly hopeless and impossible situation. I'm referring to us in our sins. How can there be a way forward for sinners when their path is blocked by what appears to be an immovable barrier? That barrier was the Red Sea for the Israelites of old. For sinners, it is the barrier of God's justice. How is it possible for sinners to enter into the promised land of heaven when God's justice demands that they be forever barred from His presence?

The answer for us is the same as it was for those ancient Israelites—God made a way! The way God made for us was the death of His Son on the cross of Calvary.

If we could only get a fuller understanding of what took place on that cross, our hearts would leap for joy and our tongues fill with praise. On the cross, Jesus so satisfied the justice of God that He removed it as our barrier.

Now the way to the Promised Land of heaven is open to us as the way to Canaan was opened when God parted the waters of the Red Sea.

How did Jesus satisfy the justice of God on the cross? He received there what that justice demanded—eternal separation from God! Imagine it! Jesus, in the space of the six hours on the cross—actually received an eternity's worth of separation from God. How can that be? It's all wrapped up in Jesus being a special man—the God-man. As such He was able to do on the cross that which no mere mortal man could do. As God in human flesh, Jesus was able to experience the wrath our sins deserve.

God's justice got its full due when Jesus died on the cross. God's justice can no longer block the way to heaven because Jesus has satisfied His righteous standards. It's important to remember that justice can only demand payment once. For justice to demand payment twice for the same offense would make justice unjust. That means this: since Jesus received on the cross the penalty for sin that justice demanded, those who are in Christ will never have to pay that same penalty.

So the great question is this: how do guilty, undeserving sinners get in Christ? And the answer is this: they do so by faith. To have what Jesus did on the cross count for us, we must come to the end of ourselves and trust completely in Him in what He did for sinners. Moses commanded the people of Israel to "stand still and see the salvation of the Lord" (v. 13). There was nothing they could do to save themselves. They could only trust in the Lord to save them. So it is with us. We can't earn our salvation or deserve it. We must rather take as our own these familiar words:

Nothing in my hand I bring,
Simply to Thy cross I cling.

The cross amounts to the crossing of the seemingly uncrossable. God's justice was the seemingly uncrossable barrier, but on the cross Jesus satisfied it or crossed it for all who believe. Those who trust in Christ will make it safely to their heavenly Canaan, never to be threatened again by the Pharaohs of this world.

December 18

Manna from Heaven

FROM GOD'S WORD, THE BIBLE...

Then the LORD said to Moses, "Behold, I will rain bread from heaven for you. And the people shall go out and gather a certain quota every day, that I may test them, whether they will walk in My law or not. And it shall be on the sixth day that they shall prepare what they bring in, and it shall be twice as much as they gather daily."

EXODUS 16:4-5

The people of Israel were out of their bondage in Egypt and in the wilderness. How were so many people to be fed? God's answer was manna, which was "a small round substance, as fine as frost on the ground" (v. 14). It is further described as being "like white coriander seed" with the taste of "wafers made with honey" (v. 31).

God had a threefold purpose in sending the manna. The first, of course, was to feed the Israelites. The second was to test them. The Lord said: "Behold, I will rain bread from heaven for you. And the people shall go out and gather a certain quota every day, that I may test them, whether they will walk in My law or not" (v. 4).

This bread from heaven would be supplied on a daily basis. It would fall during the night and the Israelites would be responsible to collect it in the morning. The only exception to this was on the seventh day, the Sabbath. The manna would not fall on the night preceding that day. The people would, therefore, have to collect enough on the previous day to last them through the Sabbath (vv. 22-30).

The people of Israel had to trust God to send the manna each night and to send them enough to carry them through the Sabbath. Would they do so?

The passage tells us that many failed the test. Some tried to save enough manna for the next day (vv. 19-20). And some went out on the Sabbath to gather it (v. 27).

The third purpose of the manna was to point them to the Lord Jesus Christ. Jesus Himself made this connection with these words: "Your fathers ate the manna in the wilderness, and are dead. . . . I am the living bread which comes down from heaven" (John 6:49, 51a).

How did that ancient manna picture the Lord Jesus? Here are some answers:

- As the manna was sent from heaven, so was Jesus.
- As the manna was mysterious (v.15), so the Lord Jesus and his salvation are beyond human comprehension.

- As the manna was small and unimpressive in appearance, so was Jesus in his humanity.
- As the manna was a gift, not created by human toil, so it is with Jesus and the salvation he came to provide.
- As the manna was for every Israelite of every state and age, so Christ is the Savior for those of every state and age.
- As the manna was pleasant to the taste and satisfying to the appetite, so the Lord Jesus is pleasant and satisfying. (Everyone who has come to know Him has found Him to be sweet to the taste and satisfying to the soul.)
- As the manna had to be personally appropriated by the Israelites, so Christ must be personally and individually appropriated by faith.
- As the manna was sufficient for the people all through their wilderness journeying, so the Lord Jesus Christ is sufficient for his people all through their pilgrim journey in this world.
- As the "mixed multitude" (unbelievers) in Israel despised the manna (Num. 11:4-6), so unbelievers despise Christ today.

No type of Christ is perfect. We must say, therefore, that while the manna prefigured the Lord Jesus in some ways, it falls short in other ways:

- The manna was physical food while Christ is spiritual food, food for the internal man.
- The manna decayed when kept; the Lord Jesus never decays.
- The manna was found only in the morning, but the Lord Jesus can be found at any time.
- The manna ceased when the people of Israel entered Canaan, but Christ will continue to be the manna on which His people will feed throughout eternity.

It isn't enough, however, to say that Christ is the manna for the Christian. We must also think about where the believer finds this manna. In other words, how does the believer feed on Christ? The answer is by looking into the Word of God where the Lord Jesus Christ is set forth.

Every Christian should take up the Word of God each morning so he or she can feed on the Lord Jesus. As we feed on the manna of the Word, we feed on the manna of the Lord Jesus.

December 19

Water from the Rock

From God's Word, the Bible...

"Behold, I will stand before you there on the rock in Horeb; and you shall strike the rock, and water will come out of it, that the people may drink."

Exodus 17:6

Not long after the Israelites crossed the Red Sea, they came to Rephidim. It was to be the place of a problem and a picture. The problem was that there was no water for them to drink. The picture was of Christ.

Their thirst was severe, so much so that the people "contended" with Moses (v. 2) and "murmured" against him (v. 3).

The anger against him was so great that Moses cried out to the Lord: "What shall I do with this people? They are almost ready to stone me!" (v. 4).

The Lord was sufficient for the occasion. He told Moses to strike a certain rock. That striking would result in enough water pouring out to quench the thirst of the multitude (v. 6). That was the picture of Christ.

Are we really supposed to see the striking of this rock as a picture of Christ? The Apostle Paul thought so, writing these words about the Israelites under Moses: "For they drank of that spiritual Rock that followed them, and that Rock was Christ" (1 Cor. 10:4).

And Jesus likened Himself to water with these words: "If anyone thirsts, let him come to Me and drink" (John 7:37).

The thirst to which Jesus referred wasn't physical in nature. It was a burning thirst to have sins forgiven and to be right with God. Only Christ can quench that thirst!

How is it that the Lord Jesus is able to satisfy spiritual thirst? It's all due to Him being smitten as the ancient rock at Rephidim was smitten by Moses.

That's what happened to Jesus on the cross. There He was, in the words of the prophet Isaiah, "Smitten by God" (Isa. 53:4).

The Son smitten on the cross by His Father! Many despise the thought. They find it repugnant. They're right to say that God the Father loved His Son, but they're wrong to assume that love made it impossible for the Father to smite His Son. They fail to see that God's smiting of His Son didn't negate His love. It was rather because of His love for His Son and for sinners.

How did the Father's smiting express love for Jesus? In this way: through that smiting, God insured that Jesus would receive such great glory that every tongue will finally confess Him as Lord (Phil. 2:11).

Through enduring the Father's smiting, Jesus would receive far more glory than He would if the smiting had never occurred.

It was also the Father's love for sinners that led to the smiting of the Son. Jesus was on that cross in a special capacity. He was there as the substitute for sinners. He was their sin-bearer (1 Peter 2:24).

Because of our sins, we deserve the eternal smiting of God. Jesus took that smiting, so we don't have to endure it.

We must understand that God wasn't being cruel to Jesus when He smote Him for our sins. Jesus didn't have to go to the cross and receive that smiting. He did it willingly, and out of love for those for whom He died.

I don't hesitate to say, then, that God specifically commanded Moses to smite the rock in the wilderness so He could picture the coming death of the Lord Jesus. How grateful we should be for that redeeming death!

Let's get back to Moses and the Israelites for a moment. Another time would come when those people would thirst again, and God would once more supply water for them from a rock. But this occasion would be different. Moses would be commanded not to strike to the rock, but rather to speak to it. And Moses, filled with anger and frustration, would strike the rock (Num. 20:1-13)

God was greatly displeased with Moses for doing that. The reason? God is very jealous of the types that He put in place of His Son's redeeming work. The smiting of the first rock was right because it pictured Christ being smitten on the cross. The second smiting was wrong because Christ was to be smitten only once for our redemption (Heb. 9:28).

The rock Moses was to smite seemed to be a very unlikely source for water, and the cross on which Jesus died seems to be a very unlikely source for spiritual life. But Moses' rock produced that water, and the cross produces that life. Christ is the greater rock who endured a far greater smiting to quench a far more serious thirst.

The Day of Atonement

FROM GOD'S WORD, THE BIBLE...

"For on that day the priest shall make atonement for you, to cleanse you, that you may be clean from all your sins before the LORD.*"*

LEVITICUS 16:30

Leviticus is a cemetery for resolutions people make to read the Bible in one year. Many start out well. Genesis is so full of interesting stories that it's easy to get through. The first part of Exodus is the same. Things begin to get a little tedious toward the end of Exodus, but readers are able to persevere. For many it all comes crashing down in Leviticus, which seems to be such a hopeless jumble of rules and regulations.

One part of Leviticus will especially come alive if we properly relate it to Christ. It is the Day of Atonement, when Israel's high priest made atonement for the sins of the people.

The high priest had to follow the clearly defined procedure laid out by the Lord. This was not his atonement. It was the Lord's.

Here are some major ways in which the work of Christ is pictured or typified by the Day of Atonement:

- The high priest alone could perform all the work on the Day of Atonement. This pictures Christ alone making atonement for His people.
- The high priest putting off his regular garments, washing himself, and putting on white linen pictures Christ laying aside His glory and being clothed in our humanity in which He was undefiled by sin (Heb. 7:26).
- The two goats, one for the sin offering and the other as the scapegoat, are types of two aspects of the work of Christ. In addition to dying as our sin offering, He also bore our sins away to such a degree that they will never be found or remembered again (Heb. 8:12).
- As the burning of the skins and flesh of the animals used for sacrifice was to be done outside the camp, so Christ went outside the city of Jerusalem to be consumed with the fire of God's wrath (Heb. 13:11-12).
- One of the most interesting aspects of the Day of Atonement has to do with the Ark of the Covenant and the mercy seat. The ark contained the tables of stone on which God had written the Ten Commandments. Those tables represented the righteous demands of God. The mercy seat was set above the ark, and was exactly the same width as the ark. When the high priest sprinkled the blood of the sacrifice on the ark, it

indicated that the blood of that innocent substitute perfectly satisfied the demands of God's law. That constitutes a beautiful picture of the cross of Christ. There Jesus shed his blood and perfectly satisfied God's demand for sinners to be punished for their sins. The law of God is perfectly satisfied by the cross of Christ.

While the Day of Atonement anticipated the work of Christ, it could only do so in an imperfect way. Here are some ways that it came short:

- Israel's high priest offered the blood of an involuntary victim, but Christ is both our high priest and our sacrifice. In other words, He, as high priest, offers His own blood as the sacrifice for His people. And He did it voluntarily.
- While the high priest had to first make atonement for himself, Jesus, as our high priest, had no sin for which to atone. He was "without blemish and without spot" (1 Peter 1:19).
- While the high priest had to make atonement for the sins of the people each year, Jesus atoned for the sins of His people once and for all (Heb. 9:25-28).
- While Israel's high priest went into an earthly sanctuary to offer his sacrifices, the Lord Jesus went into the heavenly sanctuary to make His atonement (Heb. 9:11-15, 23-24), that is, He entered into heaven as our high priest on the basis of or by virtue of His shed blood.
- While Israel's high priest went into the Most Holy Place as the representative of his people, the Lord Jesus is both the representative and forerunner of His people (Heb. 6:20). In other words, He has, as their high priest, made it possible for them to follow Him into heaven itself.

Many things in the Old Testament point us forward to the Lord Jesus, but none more so than the Day of Atonement. Those people received pardon for their sins as they looked forward in faith to the Christ who would provide full atonement. We receive that same pardon as we look backward to the Christ who has provided that atonement.

December 21

The Serpent of Brass

From God's Word, the Bible...

Therefore the people came to Moses, and said, "We have sinned, for we have spoken against the Lord and against you; pray to the Lord that He take away the serpents from us." So Moses prayed for the people. Then the Lord said to Moses, "Make a fiery serpent, and set it on a pole; and it shall be that everyone who is bitten, when he looks at it, shall live." So Moses made a bronze serpent, and put it on a pole; and so it was, if a serpent had bitten anyone, when he looked at the bronze serpent, he lived.

Numbers 21:7-9
(Read the whole passage in Numbers 21:4-9.)

Snakes! Lots of snakes! It would have been bad enough if they had just been ordinary snakes, but these were far from ordinary. They were "fiery serpents" (v. 6). Fiery serpents? Yes! Their bites burned like fire and caused death.

Where did these snakes come from? They came from God! They were His judgment on the Israelites for once again falling into the sin of complaining against Him. On this occasion, they complained about the manna with which God had been feeding them

It would seem that these people would have learned their lesson. The reason they were still eating manna is that they had grumbled about God requiring them to conquer the land of Canaan. God's judgment for that act of disobedience was to let them wander in the wilderness for forty years.

The fiery serpents certainly made for a terrible judgment. Many Israelites died from their bites.

But the same serpents that brought judgment also opened the door for God to display His grace and to point those people to the coming Christ. God's grace to the Israelites came in this form: He told Moses to make a serpent of brass, put it on a pole, and command all the people to look to that serpent for healing of the poisonous bites of those serpents. It was a matter of looking and living. So that's what those people did. They looked to the serpent on the pole and found healing. They could have refused to avail themselves of the cure because it seemed to be so absurd. Looking at a brass serpent on a pole would bring healing! There seemed to be no connection between that brass serpent and the real serpents. They could have refused the cure because it was set forth as the only cure. Imagine an Israelite saying:

"Looking at this brass serpent is too narrow and intolerant. Because there aren't a dozen cures, I refuse to accept this cure."

There's no record of the people refusing the cure on such grounds. The impression we get is that they did as God commanded. They looked and they lived.

Many people these days would be quick to dismiss this as a very strange story that has no meaning for us. The truth is that there is tremendous meaning for us in this account. You and I are here. Just as those ancient Israelites sinned against God, so we have sinned against Him. We have broken His laws time after time (Rom. 3:23). And just as God pronounced judgment upon them, so He has pronounced judgment upon us—eternal death (Rom. 6:23; 2 Thess. 1:9-10).

And something else is in this old account as well. That is God's solution. The solution for those people was a serpent of brass on a pole, and the solution for us is God's Son on a cross. There should be no doubt about the brass serpent on the pole picturing Christ on the cross because Jesus Himself made the connection in these words: "And as Moses lifted up the serpent in the wilderness, even so must the Son of Man be lifted up" (John 3:14).

There are several points of connection between that brass serpent and the Lord Jesus. God's cure for the Israelites consisted of a brass serpent that was made like the fiery serpents. God's cure for our sins is His Son, who was made a man (John 1:14; Rom. 8:3; 2 Cor. 5:21; Phil. 2:7). That brass serpent had no venom, and the Lord Jesus had no sin (2 Cor. 5:21; 1 Peter 1:19; 1 John 3:5). The brass serpent was lifted up on a pole, and Christ was lifted up on a cross. The Israelites had to look to the brass serpent to be healed, and we must look to Christ to be forgiven of our sins. As that brass serpent was the only means of healing for the Israelites, Jesus on the cross is the only means of salvation for us.

That cross seems absurd to most people these days, but it is our only hope. Jesus went there to receive the judgment that we deserve. He went there to receive an eternity of wrath for the sins of all who will trust in Him. God's call to us is to stop dismissing the cross and stop debating about it. His call to us is to look in faith to that cross for our salvation. Look and live!

The Promise of Jesus' Birth

FROM GOD'S WORD, THE BIBLE...

"Therefore the Lord Himself will give you a sign: Behold, the virgin shall conceive and bear a Son, and shall call His name Immanuel."

ISAIAH 7:14

The Lord Jesus is the theme of Scripture. He is the key to it, a gold key at that because He is of such enormous value. It can never be stressed enough that the entire Old Testament anticipates Him and His work of saving sinners. We seriously err if we think that God was trying first one plan of salvation then another during the Old Testament period. God has always had one plan of salvation, and that plan is His Son.

In the previous readings, we've concerned ourselves with people and events that point us to the Lord Jesus in one way or another. I'm likening those people and events to links in a silver chain, the chain on which we find the key of gold. The chain itself has value, but the key is of even greater value.

There are yet more links for us to treasure in the silver chain. Those links consist of the messianic promises of the Old Testament. These promises are numerous. They are also varied. In other words, they cover many of the details and aspects of the person and work of Christ.

Some of these promises pertain to the birth of Jesus. The prophet Isaiah gives us a very important detail about that birth. In the section of his prophecy that is sometimes called "The Book of Immanuel" (chapters 7-12), Isaiah informs us that Jesus would be born of a virgin (Isa. 7:14).

This promise was given to King Ahaz of Judah at a particularly tumultuous and threatening time. The Lord graciously chose to give Ahaz a sign that the threat of enemy nations would pass. A young woman, a virgin, would marry, conceive, and give birth to a son. While that child was still very young, the threat for Judah would pass. That was the meaning of Isaiah's prophecy for that time.

But in giving that promise to King Ahaz, God was giving a promise both of the birth of Jesus and the special nature of that birth. Jesus would be born, and He would be born of a virgin. The promise to Ahaz, then, had a larger meaning. How do we know it had this larger meaning? Centuries later, an angel would appear to a man named Joseph to inform him that the young woman he intended to marry was pregnant. That was no ordinary pregnancy. The angel said: "Joseph, son of David, do not be afraid to take to you Mary your wife, for that which is conceived in her is of the Holy Spirit" (Matt. 1:21).

That's not all the angel had to say. He proceeded to add that Mary's pregnancy was a fulfillment of the very prophecy that we have in Isaiah 7:14 (see Matt. 1:22-23).

The Gospel of Luke also affirms the virgin birth of Jesus. It informs us that "the angel Gabriel was sent by God. . . to a virgin betrothed to a man whose name was Joseph, of the house of David" (Luke 1:26-27). This virgin was Mary.

Gabriel appeared to Mary to tell her that she was to bear a son (Luke 1:31). She responded by asking: "How can this be, since I do not know a man?" (Luke 1:34). The angel answered by attributing her conception to the Holy Spirit (Luke 1:35).

The virgin birth of Jesus is often dismissed as being impossible. The angel who appeared to Mary dismissed those who dismiss it by saying: "For with God nothing will be impossible" (Luke 1:37).

God never takes kindly those who tell Him what He can and can't do!

Those who reject the virgin birth of Jesus would be well-advised to not set fire to the bridge over which they must cross to have salvation. If God couldn't do the virgin birth because such a thing was impossible, neither could He do the resurrection of Jesus, which would have been equally impossible. And the Apostle Paul emphatically asserts that there is no salvation for anyone if Jesus didn't come out of the grave. Paul puts it in these words: "And if Christ is not risen, your faith is futile; you are still in your sins!" (1 Cor. 15:17).

Jesus was born of a virgin, and His virgin birth was announced by the prophet Isaiah centuries before it occurred. What a marvel that is! But more marvelous than the promise of Jesus' birth is Jesus Himself, the One born to be the Savior of sinners.

December 23

The Promise of Jesus' Birthplace

From God's Word, the Bible...

"But you, Bethlehem Ephrathah, Though you are little among the thousands of Judah, Yet out of you shall come forth to Me The One to be Ruler in Israel, Whose goings forth are from of old, From everlasting."

So they said to him, "In Bethlehem of Judea, for thus it is written by the prophet: 'But you, Bethlehem, in the land of Judah, Are not the least among the rulers of Judah; For out of you shall come a Ruler Who will shepherd My people Israel.'"

Micah 5:2; Matthew 2:5-6

The precision of the Old Testament prophecies of Jesus is staggering. We have an example of that precision in Micah 5:2. Little Bethlehem would be the place of Jesus' birth.

When did Micah offer this prophecy? Do you think that perhaps he was personally acquainted with Joseph and Mary, and in personal conversation with them learned that they were about to journey to Bethlehem so he sat down and wrote his prophecy?

Brace yourself. Micah lived more than 700 years before Jesus was born! The fact that Micah knew Bethlehem would be the place of the Messiah's birth shows us that there was more at work than Micah's brain when he wrote this prophecy. God was at work with Micah. God informed Micah that Bethlehem would be the birthplace of Jesus, and Micah put pencil to paper.

It's always been fascinating to me that God chose Bethlehem as the place of Jesus' birth. Sending His Son into this world was a matter of such immense importance that we might expect it to have occurred in a prestigious city. But, no, it was Bethlehem.

Part of it had to do with the fact that Jesus was to be a descendant of David. What better place for David's greatest descendant to be born than the village where David himself was born?

Another part of it had to do with God's liking for the little. God loves the humble. He loves to yank the rug out from under men and women who strut around in pride and arrogance. The Bethlehem script offends such people. They always want God to do things in ways that rich, upper crust, highly intelligent, socially mobile people approve. God has a different agenda, saying:

I will destroy the wisdom of the wise,
And bring to nothing the understanding of the prudent.
(1 Cor. 1:19)

God's agenda is to go about His work in such a way that "no flesh should glory in His presence" (1 Cor. 1:29). Little Bethlehem would fill the bill; the grand cities of the world would not.

Those who hate the Bethlehem script think even less of the Calvary script. God sent His Son to this earth to die on a Roman cross so sinners can be made right with God and go to heaven. Proud people look with disdain upon that cross and say: "That's it? That's God way of salvation? What utter foolishness!"

But that foolishness, Paul says, is actually "the power of God and the wisdom of God" (1 Cor. 1:24). When God is being foolish, He is wiser than we are in our greatest wisdom.

That foolish cross provides salvation for sinners because Jesus received there the wrath that those sinners deserve. Because He received it, they are freed from it if they will bow in repentance and faith before the One who died on that foolish cross.

Yet another part of God's choice of Bethlehem may have been due to His desire to demonstrate the vastness of the gap that Jesus had to cross when He came to this earth. From the glories of heaven and the company of angels to the tiny village of Bethlehem, a stall, and the company of Mary, Joseph, shepherds and animals! Could there possibly be a wider gap than that?

Something of the wideness of that gap is expressed right here in Micah's prophecy. Coming to Bethlehem is One who pre-dated Bethlehem! He is the One:

Whose goings forth have been from of old,
From everlasting.

Micah's prophecy came true. Jesus was born in Bethlehem. Only those with the most obsessive hatred of Christ would bother to deny that. But being born in little Bethlehem didn't make Jesus little. He would be "Ruler in Israel" (v. 2). That doesn't mean Jesus would be the political king of the political nation Israel. His kingdom is not of this world (John 18:36). Rather, Jesus reigns over the true Israel, spiritual Israel, that consists of all those who have come to the end of themselves and have come to faith in Him.

Bethlehem was certainly little in size when Jesus was born there, but His birth has made it big. It speaks about God fulfilling with precision a centuries-old prophecy. Put that single fulfilled prophecy along with all the other Old Testament prophecies fulfilled by Jesus, and you have the truth. The Jesus of Bethlehem is the Lord of glory who came to Bethlehem to take sinners to glory.

Four Titles for Jesus

From God's Word, the Bible...

For unto us a Child is born,
Unto us a Son is given;
And the government will be upon His shoulder.
And His name will be called
Wonderful, Counselor, Mighty God,
Everlasting Father, Prince of Peace.

Isaiah 9:6

Although he prophesied many centuries before Jesus was born, Isaiah knew a lot about Christ. Those of us living on this side of Jesus' birth should know even more about Him, but that's often not the case.

As we arrive in Isaiah 9, we should be aware that we are still in that portion of Isaiah's prophecy that is often called the "Book of Immanuel." It's easy to find references to the coming Christ in this section.

I have no trouble seeing the Lord in the four titles that Isaiah uses for Him in Isaiah 9:6—Wonderful Counselor, Mighty God, Everlasting Father, Prince of Peace.

Yes, I'm aware that some regard Wonderful and Counselor as separate titles for the Lord. But since the other titles consist of two words, it makes sense to me to put Wonderful and Counselor together. When Isaiah looked down the corridor of time to see the Lord Jesus, he realized that He would be our Wonderful Counselor.

We associate counselors with keen wisdom and compassion for people.

Jesus isn't lacking in either of these essential qualifications. He is wonderful both in His wisdom and in His compassion. To say something is wonderful is to say that it evokes admiration and awe from us. Jesus is such a wise and compassionate counselor that we can only stand in awe of Him. He has perfect knowledge of both what is wrong with us and of what we should do with ourselves. His diagnosis is that we are sinners. His prescription for us is to turn to Him as our Lord and Savior. He offers this counsel to us because He cares so much for us. Wonderful counselor! That's Jesus! Wonderful in wisdom! Wonderful in compassion!

Isaiah also gives the coming Christ the title "Mighty God." The word "Mighty" carries us into the realm of warriors and war. Psalm 24:8 describes the Lord as being "mighty in battle."

As a mighty warrior, the Lord Jesus both delivers and defends His people.

We aren't by nature the Lord's people. We come into this world as part of Satan's realm. Satan is the "strong man, fully armed" who is guarding "his own palace" and keeping "his goods in peace" (Luke 11:21).

We are all in that palace and among those goods! And there we would have stayed if it hadn't been for One who is stronger than the strong man. That, of course, is Jesus. He came to this earth to defeat the strong man, and He did that by dying on the cross. Paul points to Jesus' death as the defeat for Satan and his forces by writing of Christ and His cross: "Having disarmed principalities and powers, He made a public spectacle of them, triumphing over them in it" (Col. 2:15).

Although Satan has been defeated, he is not dead. So Jesus, our mighty warrior, defends us to the point that Satan will never be able to reclaim us (John 10:28).

Isaiah also proclaims the coming Christ as our "Everlasting Father." While Jesus is the Son, and not the Father, He has the same fatherly disposition as the Father. That disposition causes Him to care for the needs of His people. Fully aware of this, the Apostle Peter urged his readers to cast their cares upon the Lord with the confidence that He cared for them (1 Peter 5:7).

The word "Everlasting" assures us that Jesus' care isn't temporary. It's not here today and gone tomorrow. It never ends.

The prophet Isaiah has yet another name for the coming Christ—"Prince of Peace," or we might say "Peaceful Prince."

This title indicates both that Jesus would exhibit peace and produce peace. It's easy to see Jesus exhibiting peace. He never seemed to be upset, anxious, tense, or on edge. He lived such a peaceful life that He was able to say to His disciples: "Peace I leave with you, My peace I give to you; not as the world gives do I give to you" (John 14:27a).

Some look at all the wars and conflicts that have occurred since Jesus came, and conclude that He couldn't possibly be the Prince of Peace. The thing they fail to see is that the peace Jesus came to provide is peace with God. We can never have true peace with others until we have peace with God, and we can only have peace with God through Jesus.

Looking ahead to Christ, Isaiah said He "shall be called" these names. I'm a fulfillment of that prophecy. I call Jesus Wonderful Counselor, Mighty God, Everlasting Father, and Prince of Peace. I hope you do as well.

December 25

The Promise of a Prophet

FROM GOD'S WORD, THE BIBLE...

"The LORD your God will raise up for you a Prophet like me from your midst, from your brethren. Him you shall hear. . . ."

"I will raise up for them a Prophet like you from among their brethren, and will put My words in His mouth, and He shall speak to them all that I command Him."

DEUTERONOMY 18:15,18

Several titles come to mind when Moses' name is mentioned: deliverer, leader, warrior, mediator, lawgiver, and judge. One title that we don't seem to associate with Moses is prophet. But Moses was a prophet. He stood before Israel as God's man to declare God's truth.

For forty years, Moses had ably led Israel. Now he was preparing to step off the stage. As he did so, his mind was drawn to the coming Messiah. Moses declared that this coming One would be a prophet like unto himself. The New Testament pointedly declares Jesus to be the fulfilment of Moses' prophecy (Matt. 21:11; John 6:14; 7:40; Acts 3:22-23).

In what ways would Jesus be a prophet like Moses? First, as Moses was sent by God, so Jesus would be. As God raised up Moses, so He would raise up Jesus.

During His earthly ministry, Jesus emphasized that He came from God. This is especially prominent in John's Gospel (John 3:16-17; 5:24,30,36,38; 6:44,57; 7:16; 8:16,18; 9:4; 10:36; 11:42; 12:45,49; 14:24; 15:21; 16:5). Jesus also made it clear that He came from God to speak for God (John 8:38;14:10,24). That's what a prophet does. He speaks for God.

The words Jesus spoke were the words of God Himself! What Jesus had to say about the sinful nature of the human heart (Matt. 15:18-19), the certainty of divine judgment (John 5:22-30), and the terrible reality of hell (Matt. 23:33; Mark 9:42-48; Luke 16:19-31) is not merely another man sharing his opinions. It's nothing less than a divine message. And what Jesus had to say about eternal salvation through His own death on the cross is also divine (John 6:47-58).

Because these truths are divine, they are certain and imperishable. We can deny them, but we can't destroy them. The course of wisdom, then, is to both recognize that Jesus spoke the words of God, and humbly submit to them. It is to do nothing less than heed the words of Moses himself: "Him you shall hear" (v. 15).

The course of wisdom is to heed this word of warning from the Lord Himself: "And it shall be that whoever will not hear My word, which He speaks in My name, I will require it of him"(v. 18).

The Pharisees of Jesus' day refused to heed His words. To them Jesus said: "He who is of God hears God's words; therefore you do not hear, because you are not of God" (John 8:47).

Another way in which Jesus would be a prophet like Moses was in faithfulness. Moses wasn't perfect in faithfulness (Num. 20:1-13), but Jesus was. As God's Prophet, Jesus never failed to accurately declare the Word of God and never failed to live up to that word which he declared.

If Jesus had not been faithful to God in every respect, He would have been a sinner Himself and couldn't have paid for the sins of others. That's how very important it is!

A third way in which Jesus would be like Moses was that He would also arise from among the people (vv. 15,18).

The prophetic office Jesus came to discharge was mediatorial in nature. He came between the holy God and sinners to make peace. In this role, it was essential for Him to be able to fully represent both parties.

Since he was already God, there was no difficulty in Him representing God. In order to represent human beings, He had to be one, too. Here is the wonder and glory of the incarnation: Jesus added to His deity our humanity so that He was at one and the same time fully God and fully man.

He couldn't have done anything for us had He not been one of us. The author of Hebrews says of Christ: "Inasmuch then as the children have partaken of flesh and blood, He Himself likewise shared in the same. . ." (Heb. 2:14).

How gracious it was of God to send His Son to take up our humanity and in that humanity to speak to us the words of eternal life! We don't appreciate to a sufficient degree what God has done to provide salvation for us.

Sent by God! Faithful like Moses! Sent as one of us! What a prophet we have in Jesus! How we should prize His prophetic work! And we prize Him in that role only if we do as Moses said, that is, hear Him. We hear Him in the reading and faithful preaching, teaching, and application of His Word, the Bible.

The Nature of Jesus

From God's Word, the Bible...

A bruised reed He will not break,
And smoking flax He will not quench;
He will bring forth justice for truth.

Isaiah 42:3

Do these verses from Isaiah really relate to the Lord Jesus Christ? The author of the first Gospel, Matthew, thought so and said so (Matt. 12:15-21). We surely wouldn't claim to know more about Jesus than one of His disciples.

Isaiah's prophecy deals with how Jesus would conduct His ministry. It must have been a precious blessing for its original readers, captives in distant Babylon. Their situation appeared to be so utterly hopeless. There seemed to be no future at all. But here was Isaiah affirming that there was a future. The Messiah would definitely come to the land of Israel, and would bring blessing both to Jews and Gentiles.

It had to be comforting to those captives to know that Christ would definitely come. It also had to be comforting to them to know that Christ would conduct Himself in a very comforting way. Isaiah's prophecy includes four blessed "nots."

The first "not" pertains to Jesus' manner of speaking:

He will not cry out, nor raise His voice. . . .
(v. 2a)

The Jews in Babylon were probably subjected to harsh speaking from their captors. The Messiah would treat His followers differently. Derek Thomas writes:

> Have you ever listened to a sergeant major drilling his men? Jesus never dealt with his disciples that way. There was no screaming or shouting of orders. He did not assume the role of a military commander.[10]

Tender gentleness would characterize Jesus and His ministry. Then we see two more "nots" in these words:

10 Derek Thomas, *God Delivers*, Evangelical Press, p. 281.

A bruised reed He will not break,
And smoking flax He will not quench.
(V. 3)

The captives in Babylon also knew what it was like to be bruised reeds and smoking flax. The reed was a shoot from a plant that could be made into a musical instrument. It would work fine until it was cracked. Then there was nothing to do except break it and throw it away.

The smoking flax referred to a candle that was so close to going out that it was producing more smoke than light.

We can all identify with these images. They picture what life is often like for God's people. Life often pounds us so much that we feel as if we have no music or light left in us.

Have you ever noticed how some people enjoy making things worse for those who are beaten down by life? They seem to delight in breaking those who are bruised, and in stamping out those who are flickering.

The Lord Jesus isn't that way with His people. He doesn't break cracked reeds. He doesn't put out flickering candles. Far from it! He actually restores His beaten people so they can make music again and glow again.

If we could ask Simon Peter about this, He would take enormous delight in affirming it is so. After his three denials of Jesus, he must have felt as if he had no more usefulness than a bruised reed or a smoking candle. But the Lord Jesus found him and restored him (John 21).

Here's the final "not" Isaiah gives us about Jesus:

He will not fail nor be discouraged,
Till He has established justice in the earth. . . .
(V. 4)

This means that the Lord Jesus would not fail to do the work that He would come to this earth to do. Part of that work, as we have been noting, was to comfort feeble people—Jesus Himself wouldn't be feeble in helping His feeble people. He wouldn't let anything throw Him off His course.

One way—the main way—Jesus would help feeble people would be the business of establishing justice in the earth. By His death on the cross, the Lord Jesus answered the demands of God's justice on behalf of His people.

As a result of Jesus satisfying God's justice on their behalf, His people would have a love for God's law in their hearts and would seek to honor that law in their conduct. Because God's people will never be perfect in this life, God's justice will never be completely established in this world. But a new world is coming! In that world all wickedness will finally be banished, and God's justice will reign (Rev. 21:8,27).

While we wait for that world, the best thing we can do in this world is proclaim our tender, comforting Christ to hearts that ache from sin.

December 27

Jesus Prophesies the Cross

FROM GOD'S WORD, THE BIBLE...

My God, My God, why have You forsaken Me?
Why are You so far from helping Me,
And from the words of My groaning?

PSALM 22:1

Of all the Old Testament prophecies about Jesus, the most detailed are Psalm 22 and Isaiah 53, and each chapter deals with the cross. That ought to underscore for us the importance of the cross, and it should be reason enough to devote one reading to each of these two splendid chapters.

One of the things that make Psalm 22 so remarkable is that it is the Messiah's own description of His crucifixion.

So the cross didn't take Jesus by surprise. He knew it was coming centuries before it came. This blows to smithereens the notion that Jesus came to this earth to set up an earthly kingdom only to have to fall back to Plan B, the cross, when the Jews rejected Him as their king.

The cross was never Plan B. The cross was in the mind and heart of God even before the world began. That's why the Bible calls Jesus "the Lamb slain from the foundation of the world" (Rev. 13:8).

How could God have planned the cross even before Adam and Eve fell into sin? The answer is that God knows the future as perfectly as He does the present or the past. Nothing ever catches Him off guard. He knew He would create this world, and He knew Adam would sin. So He had the cross ready before any of it occurred.

The fact that Jesus not only saw the cross coming but also saw the unspeakable agonies that He would have to endure there makes it all the more remarkable that He died there. He didn't have to. It was faithfulness to His Father and love for sinners that caused Him to relentlessly move toward the cross.

What were those unspeakable agonies that Jesus saw when He looked toward the cross? He mentions in this Psalm the cruel, vicious mockery that would be heaped on Him (vv. 6-8, see Matt. 27:41-43). He also mentions the thirst that He would have to endure, thirst so intense that His tongue would cling to His jaws (v. 15, see John 19:28).

The Messiah also mentions His garments being divided (v. 18), a prophecy that was minutely fulfilled (Matt. 27:35)

It's especially noteworthy that the Messiah used the word "pierced" in His description of the crucifixion. That word would become synonymous with crucifixion, but Psalm 22 was written centuries before crucifixion was ever practiced.

With the phrase "the night season" (v. 2), the Lord Jesus may very well have been anticipating the deep darkness that would fall over the land while He was on the cross (Matt. 27:45).

The greatest agony of the cross wouldn't be hearing the mockery, experiencing the thirst or seeing the soldiers dividing His garments. It wouldn't be the darkness. The greatest agony would be when Jesus, bearing the penalty for sinners, experienced in the place of those sinners the God-forsakenness that they deserve for their sins. Psalm 22 takes us to very heart of the cross in its very first words.

Yes, Jesus saw agony on the cross, and horrible agony it would be. But Jesus also saw victory, and the victory was such that it made the agony worthwhile.

Verse 21 brings us to a turning point in the psalm. The darkness lifts and the sunshine beams brightly. The storm of wrath has subsided, and all is peaceful and calm.

In the verses that remain, the Messiah rejoices that His death on the cross would not be in vain, but that it would achieve its purpose. He rejoices in the knowledge that "a posterity" will serve Him. Each generation will have those whom He purchased with His own blood to tell those in the generation following them of what He has done (vv. 30-31).

So Jesus wouldn't die on the cross with His fingers crossed, merely hoping that his death would accomplish something. That cross that He and the Father agreed upon before the world began would be effective in redeeming sinners.

As I read the Messiah's words in Psalm 22, I find myself saying with Horatius Bonar:

'Twas here the debt was paid—
Hallelujah, hallelujah!
Our sins on Jesus laid—
Hallelujah, halleljah!
So round the cross we sing
Of Christ our offering,
Of Christ our living King—
Hallelujah for the cross!

December 28

Christ, the Sin Bearer

FROM GOD'S WORD, THE BIBLE...

All we like sheep have gone astray;
We have turned, every one, to his own way;
And the LORD has laid on Him the iniquity of us all.

ISAIAH 53:6

Carried along by the Spirit of God, Isaiah saw the Lord Jesus dying on the cross, and he described what he saw in Isaiah 53. Amazingly enough, this was over 700 years before Jesus was born.

This chapter, long a favorite of the people of God, makes us wince and worship. We wince because the agony of the cross is so graphically described; and we worship because we realize that Jesus' death on the cross purchased for us forgiveness for our sins and right standing with God.

Each of the twelve verses of this chapter begs for substantial consideration, but the last sentence of the sixth verse seems to me to be the very apex of this temple of truth:

And the LORD has laid on Him,
the iniquity of us all.

There we have the nub of the matter. Jesus was on the cross in a substitutionary capacity. He was there in the place of sinners. He didn't have to be there, and once nailed to the cross, He didn't have to stay there. But He was there, and He stayed there to bear "the iniquity of us all."

The Bible uses various words to describe our condition—sin, wickedness, and transgression are words that come easily to mind. And yes, iniquity.

Iniquity! It's a foul, disgusting, revolting word. It's a nasty word to describe our nasty condition. Iniquity is twistedness. God made us a certain way, but sin has twisted us. We're not as God made us to be.

Sin is to sinful men and women a very simple thing. If God doesn't like our sin, He should just ignore it. He should just look the other way and act as if our sins don't even exist.

But what is simple to us is serious to God. The only thing that sinful men and women understand less than their sinful condition is the holiness of God. God is holy. That not only means that He is Himself free from all sin but also that He must judge our sin. For God to ignore our sin would amount to Him denying Himself. For God to ignore our sin would be equal to Him finding fault with Himself. He would be finding fault with His own holy character.

God's holiness demands that He both pronounce and carry out a just sentence upon sinners. There's no need to wait with bated breath for the sentence to be handed down. It is clearly stated in the Bible. It is everlasting separation from God. Many people say they can't understand such a harsh sentence. I can understand it. I can understand God looking upon the horror of sin and saying: "I'm not going to allow anything sinful to enter heaven. I'm not going to let sin do on the new earth what it did on the first earth."

So here we are in our sins, and here God is in His holiness! Is there any hope for us? Yes, the hope lies in the cross that Isaiah saw. That cross consisted of a special man dying a special death. When Jesus was on that cross, our sins were on Him. That's what Isaiah said to the people of faith in his day.

Jesus was on that cross as the sin-bearer. He had no sins of His own to pay for. So He could pay for the sins of others.

Unbelievers have no trouble coming up with questions. How could one man die for so many others? How could one man receive in the six hours that He was on the cross the penalty of eternal separation for our sins? The answer lies in those words "special man." Jesus wasn't a mere man; He was the God-man. So, in His death on the cross He could do things an ordinary man couldn't. As an infinite person, He could die for many others. As an infinite person, He could receive the infinite sentence of eternal wrath.

When I look at Isaiah 53, I see many important words, but I think the most precious words are the pronouns "our" and "us" and the preposition "for." It was "our griefs" and "our sorrows" that He carried with him to the cross. And it was "for our transgressions," "for our iniquities," and "for our peace" that he died (vv. 4-5). It was, my brother or sister in Christ, "the iniquity of us all" that was laid on Christ.

Bearing shame and scoffing rude
In my place condemned he stood,
Sealed my pardon with His blood;
Hallelujah! what a Savior!
(Philip Bliss)

The Resurrection of Jesus

FROM GOD'S WORD, THE BIBLE...

Therefore my heart is glad, and my glory rejoices;
My flesh also will rest in hope.
For You will not leave my soul in Sheol,
Nor will You allow Your Holy One to see corruption.
You will show me the path of life;
In Your presence is fullness of joy;
At Your right hand are pleasures forevermore.

PSALM 16:9-11

Some of David's psalms consist of two tiers. One has to do with David himself and what he was experiencing at the moment. The other level, the higher level, has to do with the Lord Jesus Christ. So it is with Psalm 16. As we read it, we can see how it applied to David. But we also get the distinct impression that the psalm is not exclusively about him. While we hear David in these verses, we seem to hear another voice as well. We especially hear that voice in the last three verses of the psalm.

We get help from Peter and Paul on this matter of identifying the other voice. They insist that the Lord Jesus is speaking in Psalm 16:9-11, and He is speaking about a matter of utmost importance, that is, His resurrection (Acts 2:25-28; 13:35).

So these verses let us hear David expressing confidence that the grave wouldn't be the end for him, and, at the same time, they let us hear the Lord Jesus saying the same.

I wonder if Jesus had these words on His mind as He came down to death's door. I wonder if He said to Himself:

Therefore, my heart is glad, and my glory rejoices;
My flesh also will rest in hope.
(V. 9)

We know that Jesus knew about His resurrection. He had predicted it on various occasions (e.g., Matt. 16:21; John 2:19-22). Jesus didn't descend into death with uncertainty and dread. The cross was something for Him to dread because it would mean being separated from God on behalf of sinners. But the grave was not something for Him to dread. The grave was merely the passageway from death to life.

Jesus would die with a glad heart because He knew about His resurrection. He would die with His "glory" rejoicing. With everything that made Him the glorious person He was, that is with His whole being, He would rejoice in His soon-coming resurrection.

Isn't it staggering that in Psalm 16 we hear the Lord Jesus expressing confidence in His resurrection hundreds of years before He came to this earth?

His confidence wasn't ill-founded or misplaced. Jesus died and was buried. And on the third day, God raised Him up. The Father, being completely satisfied with what His Son had done on the cross, refused to leave His body "in Sheol," that is, in the realm of the dead. The Father refused to allow the body of His Son to "see corruption," that is, to rot away.

In nailing Him to the cross, sinful man spoke his "truth" about Jesus. In raising Him from the grave, God spoke His truth about Jesus, and His truth showed man's "truth" to be a complete lie. The cross was man's way of saying "Jesus is a fraud." The resurrection was the Father's way of saying "Jesus is God."

There are those who say that they would like to be sure that Jesus arose from the grave. How can they not be sure? The evidence is overwhelming. The heavy stone covering the tomb was rolled away. Angels were present. The Roman guards were in a stupor. The tomb was empty. The graveclothes of Jesus were in a particularly convincing configuration. Many actually saw the risen Christ—over five hundred on one occasion (1 Cor. 15:6).

The problem with many people isn't that they can find no evidence to believe in Jesus' resurrection. It is rather that they don't want to believe the evidence because a risen Christ would put demands on them that they are unwilling to meet.

What a treasure we have in the closing verses of Psalm 16! Because Jesus spoke these words about His own resurrection, all who trust in Him as their Lord and Savior can speak them as well. So, in addition to hearing David and the Lord Jesus speak in these precious verses, I can hear yet another voice. It is my voice! Yes, I can go down to death's door with a glad heart and with my whole being rejoicing. I have the certainty that the grave is not my final home. This certainty is because Jesus said: "Because I live, you will live also" (John 14:19).

December 30

The Ascension of Jesus

FROM GOD'S WORD, THE BIBLE...

You have ascended on high,
You have led captivity captive;
You have received gifts among men,
Even from the rebellious,
That the LORD God might dwell there.

PSALM 68:18

We noted in the previous reading that some Old Testament passages move on two levels. One is the immediate level that relates to the author and what he was experiencing. The other is a higher level that finds fulfillment in the Lord Jesus Christ. It's the same with Psalm 68:18.

This sixty-eighth psalm pertains to warfare. This was something with which David was very familiar. Warfare in those days would often follow a pattern. Enemies would arise, the king of the nation would step down from his throne to lead in battle, the enemy would be defeated, captives would be taken, and the king would triumphantly return with those captives in tow to once again be seated on his throne. Furthermore, the king would often distribute the spoils of war to his subjects.

David himself followed this pattern on numerous occasions. But he also knew that there was more going on in his wars than men fighting men. Because Israel was the Lord's chosen nation, the Lord Himself would step down from His throne to defeat the enemies and triumphantly return with captives to take His throne. That's the reason the Psalm begins in this way:

Let God arise,
Let His enemies be scattered.

So the pattern we have here is coming, conquering, capturing, and conferring. The king would come to the battle, conquer and capture the enemy, and confer spoils on his people.

It's not surprising that Paul saw in David's pattern a picture of the ascension of the Lord Jesus Christ (Eph. 4:8-10). As David wrote Psalm 68:18, he himself may have also been enabled by God's Spirit to see the ascension of Jesus.

To say Jesus ascended to heaven is to say that He first descended from heaven. There was a time when the Lord Jesus rose from His throne to come to this earth. What brought Him to this earth? It was to engage in battle against the enemies of His people.

This battle took the Lord Jesus to the cross where He triumphed over Satan and his forces. Paul says of Jesus and His death on the cross: "Having disarmed principalities and powers, he made a public spectacle of them, triumphing over them in it" (Col. 2:15).

Jesus came and conquered. He came to this earth and conquered Satan just as God promised in Genesis 3:15. Matthew Henry puts it neatly, saying of Jesus: "He conquered those who had conquered us. . . ."

Having conquered, the Lord Jesus also took captives. He has "led captivity captive." Through His redeeming work on the cross, Jesus has taken all those who trust in Him out of their captivity to Satan and made them His own captives.

Many have a tendency to think that we are completely free. They like to think of themselves as standing between the Lord Jesus on one hand and Satan on the other. They tell us that they listened to the Lord Jesus state His case and then they listened to the devil state his case. Then they decided to choose Jesus, and He has been grateful to them ever since!

The Bible tells us that we always belong to a master. We are either in captivity to Satan or to Christ. When the Lord Jesus saves us, He takes us out of captivity to Satan and makes us His captives. But in wonderful irony, captivity to Christ makes us truly free (John 8:32). Ask a Christian if he is a captive, and he will say "Yes!" Ask him if he is free, and he will say "Yes!"

Because of His victory on the cross, the Lord Jesus has won spoils that He now lavishes on His people—marvelous privileges and advantages. He showers them with "every spiritual blessing" (Eph. 1:3).

Our need is to get a better understanding of Jesus' work on our behalf. He rose from His throne in glory to come down to this earth and even down to the grave itself so that He could take us out of captivity to Satan and make us His captives. After descending to this earth, Jesus ascended to heaven again (Acts 1:9-11). From there He pours out His gifts on His people.

We who have become His captives by His atoning death on the cross now glorify our ascended Christ who daily blesses us. And we look forward to that day when our ascended Lord will descend once more to take us to share His eternal glory.

December 31

The Gospel Reign of Jesus

From God's Word, the Bible...

The Lord said to my Lord,
"Sit at My right hand,
Till I make Your enemies Your footstool."
The Lord shall send the rod of Your strength out of Zion.
Rule in the midst of Your enemies!

Psalm 110:1-2

No list of Old Testament prophecies of Christ is complete without Psalm 110, which is quoted more than any other in the New Testament.

I wonder what David was thinking as he wrote the words of verses 1 through 4. He had to know that they weren't just his words. He had to realize that he was being prompted to write words that were being given to him by God's Spirit. And what words! In these verses, David actually reports the words spoken by the Lord to the Lord!

Who are these Lords (v. 1)? The first is God the Father; the second is God the Son.

In the writing of this psalm, God's Spirit carried David all the way from the humiliation of Christ to His exaltation, that is, all the way from Jesus coming to this earth as a man to Him returning to heaven. The Spirit carries David from Jesus' descending to His ascending. Quite a tour!

What did David hear the Father saying to the Son? We can capture it in the words "Sit" (v. 1), "Rule" (v. 2) and "You are" (v. 4).

The Father saying "Sit" to the Son would mean that redemption's work was now done. The agonies of the cross would be in the past. The grave would be defeated. With it all accomplished and over, the Father offers the Son the position of highest honor in heaven—the seat at His, the Father's, right hand.

The Father, fully satisfied with the redeeming work of His Son, has determined that He should have preeminence in all things (Col. 1:18).

If we want to be pleasing to God, we must seek to give Jesus the preeminence in our thinking, speaking, and doing. And we must give Him preeminence in our public worship. How sad it is that this needs to be said about worship, but our days make the saying of it essential.

With the word "Rule," the Father would be telling His Son to begin His gospel reign. We must not think that Jesus' rule is something that will occur at the end of time. Jesus is ruling now.

One of the things we need to note about this gospel reign is that it will finally result in the complete subjection of all the Messiah's enemies (v. 1). Every knee will finally bow before him and every tongue will finally confess that he is Lord (Phil. 2:9-11).

A second thing for us to note is that Jesus' reign is conquering enemies even now. As the church preaches the gospel, the Lord Jesus Christ extends his "rod" or scepter "out of Zion" (v. 2).

Here's another thing: Jesus' gospel reign is manifested by the people of God themselves. We don't have to be in the courts of heaven to see Jesus reigning. We see that reign every time a sinner is conquered by the gospel of Christ. How are sinners so conquered? By the Lord making them willing to receive the gospel! Thus the Father says to the Messiah:

Your people shall be volunteers
In the day of Your power. . . .
(V. 3)

When the gospel exerts its conquering power, those who receive it begin to display "the beauties of holiness" (v. 3). Every sign of holiness among God's people is evidence that the gospel reign is in effect. That's no small thing because those saved in the gospel age will be as numerous as the drops of dew that come "from the womb of the morning" (v. 3).

With the words "You are," the Father accentuates the priestly work of King Jesus. The king is also a priest!

This dual role, as noted earlier in these readings, was pictured by Melchizedek, who was both a king and a priest in Abraham's day (Gen 14:18-20). While he was associated with both righteousness and peace, Melchizedek couldn't perfectly represent those things. But Jesus does.

The way by which he produced peace between guilty sinners and the holy God was through righteousness. He Himself lived a perfectly righteous life, providing the righteousness that we do not have, righteousness that is credited to us when we believe. Furthermore, Jesus' death also had to do with righteousness. He died to receive the righteous sentence of the holy God against our sins. In other words, He received on the cross what God's righteousness demanded, namely, the wrath of God.

David was certainly blessed to write these words, and we are certainly blessed to read them. And we are even more blessed if we find that we are truly subjects of the King, rescued from the power and dominion of sin, forever to love, serve, and obey Him. Is He your Lord and King?

Books Included in this Series

My Coffee-Cup Meditations includes the following

A Dog and A Clock (Series#1)

The "Thumbs-Up" Man (Series#2)

When God Blocks Our Path (Series#3)

Fading Lines, Unfading Hope Series#4)

The Day the Milk Spilled (Series#5)

"Where Are the Donuts?" (Series#6)

Sure Signs of Heavenly Hope (Series#7)

My Dog Knows It's Sunday (Series#8)

Rover and the Cows (Series#9)

Apples of Gold in Silver Settings (Series#10)

Old Houses, New Houses (Series#11)

Golden Key and Silver Chain (Series#12)